Storage:
Cabinets,
Closets and
Wall Systems

Storage: Cabinets, Closets and Wall Systems

by Jane Randolph Cary

Drawings by
Lloyd Birmingham
Richard Meyer
Eugene Thompson

POPULAR SCIENCE BOOKS

ISBN: 0-943822-50-5

Seventh Printing, 1985

Manufactured in the United States of America

Contents

ACKNOWLEDGMENTS

Special thanks go to Sandy Rabinowitz, The Bank Street Carpenter, for his advice and guidance in the preparation of this book, and to my editor, Henry Gross, for his many helpful thoughts and concerned editing of the manuscript.

For their interest and cooperation in supplying information and illustrative material, I am sincerely grateful to the following retailers and manufacturers:

Black & Decker Inc.
Coastal Abrasive & Tool Company
Comark Plastics Division
Duo-Fast Corporation
Du Pont Company
Formica Corporation
Freedman Artcraft Engineering
General Products Company, Inc.
Haas Cabinet Company, Inc.
HB Fuller Company

Hardwood Plywood Manufacturers Association
Klise Manufacturing Co.
Leigh Products Inc.
M. Wolchonok & Son, Inc.
Prestigeline Inc.
Rohm & Haas
Slater Electric Inc.
Stanley Hardware Division
Swingline Inc.
William Hunrath Co., Inc.

Preface

MOST PEOPLE FEEL there's one luxury on a par with having money in the bank — having plenty of storage space. Given the ever-increasing number of possessions we accumulate and the limited space we have to store them, it's no wonder we dream of mansion-sized closets and built-ins — even though the places we live in aren't elastic.

Since in reality we are all stuck with nonflexible houses, the solution to the storage problem is to make the spaces we have hold more. How? By compartmentalizing closets, organizing the clutter in basements and attics, hanging more shelves, building a wall system or two. In short, by putting wasted space to work we can increase by 40 to 50 percent the total storage capacity of a home or apartment.

If, for instance, you want more closets but have no room to build new ones, revamp the old ones. Enlarging the opening and installing bi-fold doors will make the interiors and contents more accessible. But more important, all the wasted space overhead, on floors, and in corners can be recaptured and used to the fullest.

Walls have enormous storage potential for systems of shelves and cabinets. There are dozens of ideas in this book to help you utilize this space effectively.

Walls and old closets are just two of the potential storage spaces most often overlooked. This book highlights others in attics, basements, garages, in kitchens and baths, in living rooms and dens. There are ideas and projects for these and other situations; for creating the kind of storage you need, where you need it. Some projects are designed to suit specific purposes; others are general-purpose structures which can be adapted to your specific needs. Construction details and procedures are given for each of the projects here. While no book can be tailored to fit every contingency or personal preference that's likely to arise, the approach and materials are all basic ones which you can augment or revise according to your own habits and experience.

1 | Construction Materials

ALL THE CABINETS, closets, and shelves in this book are fashioned of softwood lumber in ready-to-use stock sizes and the plentiful plywoods whose quality and grade combinations help you control costs and get a job done quickly.

Time is a big motivator when it comes to building new places for storage. Your possessions either are becoming too hard to find once stored away or they are pushing you out of the house. Something must be done, and the faster the better.

Of course, there are plenty of ready-built storage structures you can buy in five minutes. But they are expensive and, being mass-produced, are made in standard sizes that often limit where you can put them and what you can store in them.

Whether it's books, clothing, gardening tools, or ski poles that are cluttering your life, there in the nearest lumberyard are the 2x4s, 1x10s, and plywood sheets ready to help organize them all.

LUMBER AND PLYWOOD. Choose clear, unblemished, more expensive stock only when appearance will be an important factor in the finished project. Or, where stability will be crucial, as for example, the finish framing around a closet opening that will be fitted with bifold doors, as shown in Chapters 9 and 10 (knots or warp impair smooth operation of the doors).

Select lesser grades of stock lumber and plywood for basement, garage, and attic projects, such as those in Chapters 16, 17, and 18. They are designed to utilize inexpensive material yet be sturdy and serviceable.

Also, make it a point to choose basic material according to how you plan to final-finish any given project. A general rule to follow is:

Select better grades of lumber if you'll be using a clear or natural-stain finish. Choose more economical grades if the project will be painted.

Select softwood plywood if the project will be painted.

Select hardwood plywood of good quality if you plan to use clear finishes. It will cost more but you'll have less work to do in the final-finishing stage.

Consider, too, how you want to spend your time in relation to the effort it takes to treat and fill defects in cheaper grades of material. Some craftsmen delight in buying up bargains that will yield worthwhile sections after holes, splits, pitch-pockets are cut away. Others find this a tedious chore and prefer to get on with the actual building.

Selecting material wisely includes buying the quality grades and kinds of wood that will do the best job at the lowest cost. Another is dealing with a reputable supplier, one who is knowledgeable about the product he sells and who will take the time to discuss a project with you. Finding and cultivating this kind of business relationship cannot be done overnight, however. The upsurge in the do-it-yourself market has put limits on the amount of personal service any given customer can receive, especially on a busy weekend. Moreover, there are people getting into the active retail lumber business who often know less about judging stock quality than their customers do.

In view of these conditions, be guided in your purchases by what you can see and, in general, by lumber grading systems established to rate quality features according to price and performance. Since there is one grading system for softwood lumber, and one for softwood plywood, and another for hardwood plywood, and yet another for redwood, a handy reference list will be easier to consult when needed than trying to memorize the combinations of facts and features involved in each. The charts on the following pages are offered for your convenience.

NOMINAL AND ACTUAL SIZES
OF SOFTWOOD LUMBER

NOMINAL	ACTUAL	NOMINAL	ACTUAL
1x2 inches	$^3/_4$x1$^1/_2$ inches	2x2	1$^1/_2$x1$^1/_2$
1x3	$^3/_4$x2$^1/_2$	2x3	1$^1/_2$x2$^1/_2$
1x4	$^3/_4$x3$^1/_2$	2x4	1$^1/_2$x3$^1/_2$
1x6	$^3/_4$x5$^1/_2$	2x6	1$^1/_2$x5$^1/_2$
1x8	$^3/_4$x7$^1/_4$	2x8	1$^1/_2$x7$^1/_4$
1x10	$^3/_4$x9$^1/_4$	2x10	1$^1/_2$x9$^1/_4$
1x12	$^3/_4$x11$^1/_4$	2x12	1$^1/_2$x11$^1/_4$

Order lumber by nominal size and actual lengths. Specify smooth or rough surfacing.

The most widely available softwoods are pine, fir, cedar, cypress, hemlock, spruce, redwood.

Larger sizes, 4x4 up to 8x8-inch lumber, are not required for most storage projects, so are not listed. Standard lengths for lumber are 8, 10, 12, 14, 16, 18, 20, and 24 feet.

SOFTWOOD LUMBER GRADING

SELECT OR CLEAR (nominal thickness of 1 inch)		COMMON (nominal thickness of 1 inch)		DIMENSION LUMBER LIGHT FRAMING (nominal thickness 2 inches)	
Category	Remarks	Category	Remarks	Category	Remarks
A	No blemishes. Ideal for natural finishes.	No. 1	Larger tight knots than grade at left. OK for painting.	Construction	Use where very sturdy framing is needed
B	Tiny blemishes. Fine for natural finishes.	No. 2	More knots; some loose. Can be painted.	Standard	Just as good as the above for closet framing
C	Some small blemishes and tight knots. Fine for natural finishes and for paint.	No. 3	Has splits and holes. Do not consider for painting.	Utility	Not for closet framing but suitable for cabinets and other small projects
D	Several small knots. OK for painting.	No. 4	Many splits and holes. Some sections can be salvaged. Do not paint.	Economy	Avoid for storage projects
		No. 5	Unsuitable for these storage projects.		

SOFTWOOD PLYWOOD GRADING

A	Smooth surface, tiny blemishes are neatly repaired. Ideal for painted finish; suitable for natural finishes.	
B	Smooth, firm surface with small repair plugs and tight knots. Suitable for painting, but not suggested for clear finishes.	
C	Rough, unrepaired knotholes. Do not attempt to paint. Suitable for areas that will not show.	
D	Large rough knotholes. Use only where appearance and strength are not important factors.	

The most popular and widely available softwood plywood face veneers are pine, fir, spruce, hemlock. When ordering specify kind of wood surface veneer, surface grade of face, surface grade of back, thickness.

HARDWOOD PLYWOOD GRADING

Premium (sometimes referred to as A)	Beautifully matched grain and color. No blemishes. Ideal for natural finishes. Very expensive. Not widely available, though can be specially ordered.
Good (1)	Color and grain are fairly well matched. Ideal for natural finishes. Expensive but worth it for favored projects.
Sound (2)	Smooth, solid surface with some small, tight knots. Suitable for painting or natural finishes.
Utility (3)	Rough; small splits. Has knotholes. Is not suitable for painting.
Backing (4)	Very rough surface, large holes, other defects. Not for these storage projects.

The most popular hardwood surface veneers are ash, birch, cherry, hickory, mahogany, maple, oak, poplar, walnut. When ordering specify kind of face veneer wood, surface grade of face, surface grade of back, thickness, and core material.

Grading systems and the descriptive words in charts provide some clues to material quality, but not all of them. Judgments based upon what your eyes, nose, and hands can tell you are also important. While this kind of expertise comes with practice, and some trial and error, there are quality features you can see and feel. For example, such defects as splits, checks, knots, holes, dark spots, pitch pockets are visible and if not too extensive can be cut out, filled in, or covered up without damaging the usefulness of the material.

Moisture is the real tripper in selecting lumber because you cannot see whether the wood is as dry as it ought to be. It may

CORE MATERIALS OF HARDWOOD PLYWOOD

CORE TYPE	THICKNESS RANGE	CHARACTERISTICS
Veneer core	$1/8''$ to $3/4''$	Good screw-holding power Moderate cost Exposed edges difficult to stain Doors of it are susceptible to warpage Difficult to machine
Lumber core	$5/8''$ to $3/4''$	Easy to machine Solid edges easy to stain, trim Holds butt-hinges well Most expensive
Particleboard	$5/8''$ to $1''$	Very stable Least expensive Panel is very heavy Edges difficult to stain Poor edge-holding power
Fiberboard	$5/8''$ to $1''$	Very stable Moderate cost Panel is very heavy Exposed edges easy to stain Easy to machine

Courtesy Hardwood Plywood Manufacturers Association

REDWOOD GRADING

HEARTWOOD	SOME SAPWOOD°	EVALUATION
Clear all-heart	Clear	Exceptional quality. Expensive. Not necessary for storage projects.
Select heart	Select	Small blemishes; very durable.
Construction heart	Construction common	Larger knots than above.
Garden heart	Merchantable	Many large knots. May be suitable for some garage, basement projects.

°Sapwood grade has light streaks (as opposed to Heartwood, which is uniform in coloring) but is suitable for storage projects and is less expensive generally.

shrink, or distort, after you get it home—houses are warmer and drier than lumberyards.

In theory, lumber is supposed to be sufficiently seasoned before it goes on the market; either by air-drying or kiln-drying. But in these days of demand for more, more, the time-consuming seasoning process is apt to be rushed a little. Go with caution. Some canny consumers claim they can tell unseasoned lumber by its odor. It smells green, they say, and wet. Others go by touch. One test is described this way: Hold the board between both hands, palms flat. Press tightly for five or six seconds. Dry lumber will begin to feel warm—and dry. Green lumber will always feel cool and clammy.

Another wary shopper claims success with this approach: Sprinkle a little sawdust on the board and blow it off. Sawdust clings to green lumber; on dry lumber it skitters off as though alive. Other wise shoppers sight down the surfaces and along the edges of a length of lumber to check for evidence of warp.

Grain pattern direction is another clue to how likely a board will warp. Notice the grain lines in the cut end of the board. The methods used to cut a log into lumber produce what is called vertical or flat grain patterns. A board with vertical, or slightly diagonal, striations is less apt to change shape later than one having flat, or horizontal, grain lines.

Most dealers will cut material for you, for a fee, provided you order whole-number straight cuts. (Make sure your own measurements are correct, and that the cut is made on the waste side of the cutting line, to allow for the kerf.) Then recheck the measurements of the cut material before you take it home.

If you need fractional lengths or shaped cuts, order material to the nearest whole-size that permits you to do your own final cutting with the least amount of waste.

Cutting and drilling plywood to avoid splintering its thin surface veneers takes special care. The surface is less likely to be damaged if the saw blade's cutting strokes *enter the face* of the veneer. Splintering will occur if the cutting strokes *exit through the back* of the veneer. In other words, have the good veneer side *down* if you're using a saber or portable power saw; their teeth cut on the upward stroke. Have the good side *up* if you're using a crosscut, radial arm, or table saw; their teeth cut on the downward stroke.

When drilling plywood, avoid damage and splintering by stopping the bit just before it breaks through the surface ply. Complete the hole by drilling into it from the opposite side. Another technique is to drill through one side and on into a piece of wood that has been securely clamped to the back of the material.

PROCESSED WOODS. Man-made materials are worth considering in some storage projects because they are durable and as a rule less expensive than lumber or plywood.

Hardboard is a dense, tough sheet material that's available in $^1/_8$-inch or $^1/_4$-inch thicknesses. It is suitable for cabinet backs, drawer bottoms, small sliding doors on cabinets. The $^1/_4$-inch material can be used for shelves provided there are supports every 24 inches or so. Since hardboard is thin and brittle, it can't be end-fastened or joined in the ways lumber can. Instead, fasten wood blocks to the material where joints are needed. If you plan to paint hardboard, give it a coating of primer-sealer first.

Particleboard (aka pressboard, chipboard) comes in 4x8 sheets and in thicknesses of from $^1/_4$ inch up to and including $1^7/_8$ inches. Half-inch particleboard is suitable for shelves and large sliding doors for cabinets. Thinner material is useful as cabinet backing, drawer bottoms, and small sliding doors. Its natural color ranges from dull tan to monotonous amber. However, in recent years particleboard has become more attractive. You can buy it in sheets that are clad in bonded-on vinyl woodgrain and solid-color finishes. Immediately, you have a material that is not only better looking, but one that doesn't need much final-finishing. Most home centers and building-supply dealers stock these prefinished sheets or can easily order them for you.

Most precut, prepackaged shelving sold in shelf shops is of vinyl-clad particleboard. Some packagers even offer color-coordinated shelves, brackets, and standards in blue, yellow, orange, red, and white, as well as light and dark wood tones. As the core material between hardwood veneers the uses for particleboard become even broader: shelves, cabinet tops and doors having the look of expensive cherry or walnut but not the cost.

Because particleboard is made of bits of wood, sawdust, and resins compacted together under heat and pressure, it is very heavy. It's also difficult to cut; saw blades dull in no time. It has poor

edge-holding power for fasteners; joints and seams need reinforcing with wood blocks. Nails, screws, or bolts should be used
in combination with glue. It takes paint well, but do not use
water-based ones; the water will eventually cause the wood par-
ticles to expand. To treat and finish its bristly rough edges, apply a
paste filler, sand smooth, and add paint, edging tape, or molding
strips of wood, metal, or plastic.

PLASTICS. Although wood is the basic structural material for
storage projects in this book, today's innovative plastics have features and qualities you can use to advantage for cabinets and
countertops, shelves, sliding doors, drawer fronts, cubes, and
boxes.

In addition to being waterproof and impervious to many substances that stain or damage wood, plastics don't need to be
sanded or treated with fillers and sealers. What's more, since color
and texture are manufactured into the material, painting, stain-
ing, varnishings are final-finishing steps you can also skip.

From an appearance standpoint, plastics combine well with natural wood tones. Both opaque and translucent ones give a project
a contemporary look when used as sliding doors or drawer fronts.
Cabinet tops of thick $3/_4$-inch marble-like acrylic sheet material
blend appropriately with traditionally styled pieces whether they
are true antiques or reproductions.

But even more important is the hard, durable, nonporous nature
of this material which resists the splintering and shattering commonly associated with wood, glass, and marble.

Corian®. This is a thick acrylic sheet material having delicate
drifts of color running all the way through it as natural marble has.
Though in appearance it is as opalescent as a cameo, Corian is
heavy, tough, non-porous, and resistant to a wider variety of stains
than either wood or the plastic laminates. It is ideal for cabinet
and counter tops. Stock panel sizes are 98 inches, 121 inches,
and 145 inches in length. Widths are generally 30 inches, but
you can have most any dimension you want; the dealer will cut
the material to size for you. There may be a cutting charge but
the waste portions will belong to you. Take them; this material
makes ideal windowsill covering. Or a waste piece may be just
right for a small shelf, or cabinet top, or door threshold. Corian

sheet comes in $1/4$-inch, $1/2$-inch, and $3/4$-inch thicknesses. The thinner material is ideal for backsplashes, protective wall covering (behind a sink, for example), and for drawer fronts.

Before you accept an order, check the panel's edges for evidence of damage. The material comes with a peel-off protective film on the face side. This covering must be removed before any cutting is done.

In making straight cuts, use a portable circular saw with carbide-tipped blade (10 teeth).

Curved cuts are best done with a saber saw using a wood-cutting blade (10 teeth).

Drill with a power drill using a hole saw, spade drill, or $1/4$-inch twist drill depending on the size of the opening needed. Holes for screws should be $1/64$-inch oversize to allow for expansion and contraction and to prevent pressure-cracking.

Shaped edges can be made with a trim router and decorative router bits.

Edge-finishing—rounding-off corners, smoothing away tool cut-marks—is done with an electric sander using 320-grit paper, or by hand with 320-grit paper wrapped around a sanding block. Then, buff lightly with 3M Scotch Brite wiping pad to match edge gloss with surface gloss.

Flat sections of countertop panels, backsplash strips, and edge-facing strips must all be butt-jointed together rather than mitered or rabbeted. Joints are fastened with a compound such as G.E. translucent white silicone sealant applied with caulk gun. Use panel adhesive to fasten the countertop to the wood support strips of the cabinet. Clamp with masking tape to allow adhesive time to set up.

Wear safety glasses, gloves, and shoes when cutting and drilling—and carrying Corian; work in the open if at all possible; wear a dust mask when cutting and drilling indoors. Ear muffs or plugs are recommended for your comfort when using circular saw and router. This is an equally good idea for all cutting operations whether on wood, metal, or plastics.

These are just some of the important factors involved in handling and installing Corian panel material. As with any material you would like to use but have little experience with, be guided by the manufacturer's recommendations.

Plexiglas®. Also an acrylic sheet material, Plexiglas is sold in large hobby and crafts shops, as well as in hardware, glass, and building supply stores. It is sold by the square foot, comes in $^1/_8$-inch, $^3/_{16}$-inch, and $^1/_4$-inch thicknesses, and in general is cut to size while you wait. These are straight cuts only, however. Any special cutting, odd sizes or shapes are steps you can do yourself with regular hand and power tools. If in-store cutting results in waste pieces being left over, take them for use in smaller projects later.

Range of colors and textures is broad. There is clear transparent material as well as smooth-surfaced translucent sheet which comes in twenty-five colors plus nine densities of white. Standard opaque and semi-opaque colors include white, black, brown, mustard. Transparent colors include blues, reds, yellows, greens plus five densities of gray and five of bronze.

Textured surfaces abound, from smooth matte to dense stipple and waffle-like patterns. One, called Flair DP-32 ripple-textured Plexiglas, comes in thirteen rich stained-glass colorings and is ideal for backlighted cabinet doors, or for sliding doors.

Plexiglas comes with a heavy peel-off paper covering which you leave intact while cutting, drilling, and edge-sanding. The material is worked much like wood and soft metals.

Curved cuts, for example, are made with saber, band, or reciprocating jig saw. Use finetooth blades—14 teeth per inch for $^3/_{16}$-inch and $^1/_4$-inch material; 32 teeth per inch for $^1/_8$-inch material. Band saws should have at least 10 teeth per inch.

There are a number of ways to make straight cuts. Use a scribing tool much like a glass cutter, place the scribed line over a $^3/_4$-inch dowel and press downward on both sides of the line to make a smooth break in the material. Two cutting tools are available at hardware stores and plastics-supply dealers: the Plastic Plus Cutting Tool, or the Red Devil Cutting Tool For Plexiglas.

Straight cuts can also be made with a saber saw by guiding the tool along a straightedge. Circular saws are also ideal for straight cutting. There are blades made for the purpose such as the Cope RH-600 or RH-800 Circular Saw Blade For Plexiglas. Or you can use a steel crosscut blade which is recommended for finish cuts on plywood, veneers, laminates. Blades should have at least 6 teeth per inch and be uniform in shape, height, and distance from point-to-point.

Drilling can be done with a standard twist hand drill commonly used for metals. With power drill, a special drill bit is used. Plexiglas manufacturer recommends specially ground Hanson Special Purpose High Speed Twist Drills.

Edge-finishing is relatively simple and is done in three stages: smooth finish, satin finish, transparent finish.

To smooth-finish, for rounding-off corners and smoothing uneven cuts, use medium- to fine-tooth metal files. Saw, file, and other tool marks can be removed by scraping the edge with a sharpened piece of metal such as the back of a hacksaw blade. Or you can smooth-finish by sanding with medium grit (60-80) production paper.

Satin-finishing further improves the appearance of the edge, but more important, prepares it for cementing. Sand with increasingly finer grits (150-320) wet-or-dry paper. Where such finished edges will be bonded together, do not round-off the edges because this will cause bubbles in the cemented joint.

Transparent-finishing produces a high-gloss edge that contributes to a sleek final-finished appearance. Use fine grit (400-500) wet-or-dry paper, then buff with clean muslin wheel dressed with a good grade of fine grit buffing compound.

Joining is done with specially formulated cements which create transparent joints. The principle involved in making the butt joints is easy to master provided you use the proper cements and applicators suitable for the type, or grade, of the material. There are two formulations of Plexiglas generally available at retail: Plexiglas G (general purpose) and Plexiglas K, a safety glazing grade. The only significant difference between the two is that K must be worked with a thickened cement while G can be joined with substances that are almost water-like in consistency. For instance, with Plexiglas G use IPS Weld-On #3 Solvent For Cementing Plexiglas; methylene chloride "MDC"; ethylene dichloride "EDC"; or 1-1-2 trichloride. Apply the solution to the joint with Hypo RE-200 Applicator, always keeping the cement joint horizontal.

Thickened cements, such as IPS Weld-On #16 Cement For Plexiglas, produce a stronger joint. While it can be used with Plexiglas G, it is the only recommended cement for use with Plexiglas K. Textured panels cannot be cemented, but can be held in grooved channels or by molding strips.

Heat bending is another unique method of handling and shaping this material. With a strip heater, which you can make yourself, sheet can be bent along a straight line and set in any desired angle.

Do not heat this material in the oven or with an open flame. It is a combustible thermoplastic and should be treated as an ordinary combustible substance such as wood. Like wood, it will ignite and burn if placed in an open flame or in contact with any other source of ignition. Observe fire precautions appropriate for comparable forms of wood or paper products. The sheet softens at temperatures ranging from 290°F to 340°F. In storage or use, Plexiglas should not be exposed to temperatures above 180°F.

Du Pont's Lucite® and Polycast® by Polycast Technology Corporation are two other brands of acrylic sheet material that can be shaped and worked in the same manner as Plexiglas. You'll find them in hobby shops, home centers, plastics supply, and most building supply stores.

LAMINATES AND OTHER PLASTICS. There are few surfaces that cannot be made more serviceable or attractive with plastic laminate sheet material. Certainly they are ideal for hosts of storage projects: cabinets, shelves, door and drawer fronts, countertops, wall systems.

Whether you want to laminate a single shelf or sink countertop, the techniques for applying the material are the same. The tools you'll need are the basic hand and power tools most home carpenters already own. There are some specialized ones the pros use that make the job easier: a flameless heater to facilitate curve bending; laminate cutting shears. You can find them in better hardware stores and at laminate supply shops.

One of the keys to successful laminating is the core material you use. Choose good quality plywood or particleboard that's firm, straight, free of splits. All small dents or holes must be filled and sanded smooth.

You can cut plastic laminate sheet to size with a hacksaw or fine-tooth handsaw. If you use either of these, cut the laminate with its face-side up. You can also use a saber saw with fine-tooth wood-cutting blade (have face side of the laminate down). A table saw with carbide-tipped blade is also satisfactory; have face side of laminate up, when cutting. Or, you can use the manually operated laminate shears that pros use to make straight as well as shaped cuts very quickly.

In bonding laminates to the core material, use contact cement formulated for this purpose. Use a short-nap paint roller, then a notched spreader. For laminating small surfaces, like a drawer front or face edging, apply the cement with an animal hair paintbrush.

To eliminate air pockets and assure a complete bond, the newly applied laminate should be rolled, or pressure-pressed, all over. For this you can use an ordinary rolling pin, but hammering on a short hardwood block guided over the laminate does a better job, especially for edging strips. At critical joints where surface sheet and edging strips meet, a J-roller helps assure a tight, reliable bond.

To trim excess laminate from overhangs and at corners, use a power router fitted with a straight cutter. (To prevent laminate being scorched, coat cutting area with petroleum jelly.) Trimming can also be done with an ordinary block plane. To bevel edges neatly and professionally cut either with a router and bevel cutter, or by hand using a smooth file.

An excellent booklet, well illustrated and filled with clear, easy-to-follow tips and instructions for plastic laminate applications, is available at Formica Brand laminate dealers for just 25 cents.

Other forms of plastic materials, vinyl and polyester for instance, are bonded to thin core materials to form ready-to-use linings for cabinets, drawers, bookcases. You are also familiar with similar materials used on bathroom walls and tub surrounds. These generally are brittle and difficult to cut without chipping surface edges. Also seams have to be butt-joined and covered with metal or vinyl strips. But the material does provide cabinet interiors and backings that are durable, attractive, and maintenance-free.

Another lining material is melamine component panel (MCP), a product of Formica Corporation. It is used for vertical surfacing inside closets, base and wall cabinets, and as backings for shelf systems.

It comes in 4x8 sheets, $^3/_8$-inch or $^3/_4$-inch thick, and consists of decorative and colorful melamine (the kind dishes are made of) thermal-fused to a core of particleboard or fiberboard. It can be worked like wood—sawed, drilled, routed, shaped, and joined —using ordinary hand and power tools, though a router with carbide bit is recommended for trimming, shaping, and beveling. As for fasteners, nails or wood screws used in combination with glue are suggested.

Exposed edges can be finished with tapes or laminated moldings that match MCP patterns and colors. MCP is intended only for interior use on vertical surfaces or light-duty horizontal ones, and in storage units whose interiors you want to be smooth, colorful, and easy to keep clean. MCP is available in woodgrain finishes as well as solid colors developed to coordinate with Formica's decorative laminate sheet material.

2 | Finishes that Last

EACH OF THE materials you'll be working with—softwood lumber, softwood plywood, hardwood plywood, and fir-surfaced plywood—has characteristics that call for different finishing methods. This is especially true of fir-surfaced plywood, a softwood material but one that needs specialized handling nonetheless.

What's more, the kind of finish you give a project should also be influenced by the decor and furnishings in any given room. Choose colors and finishes that work well with the wood tones and hues already present.

It's tempting to choose only natural finishes and stains because they are quick and easy to use, or because they highlight the grain of the wood. But look at the shades of wood around you in furniture or even woodwork. There's deep walnut perhaps, or warm cherry, dark mahogany, pale or bleached modern-looking wood. Will the stain on softwood match or blend well? It's unlikely. In such cases paint, either high or semigloss enamel that matches wall or woodwork color, may be a wiser choice.

In kitchen and bathrooms, on the other hand, the natural and clear finishes, as well as painted ones, look well when used according to the style and predominant color in these areas.

For basements, garages, and attics, storage units that are strictly utilitarian need not be given any special final finish. Just sand and coat with a clear sealer to control splinters and protect the wood from dirt.

Paints most suitable for shelves and cabinets are the alkyd enamels—either high-gloss or semigloss. The urethanes (plastic paints) are another good choice because of their elasticity and abrasion resistance. Also the very slick, very hard epoxy paints are super-serviceable though tricky to work with since they dry so quickly. Latex paints are not as sturdy as those mentioned above, and since storage places get hard wear, these coverings should be considered last.

For clear and natural-stain finishes choose shellac, varnish, polyurethane varnish, or penetrating resins—whichever type you are most comfortable working with.

Often, antiquing paints with their dark-toned wipe-off glazes give shelves and cabinets just the right color toning that stain or paint alone cannot accomplish. Consider these if a stain would look too raw or a paint too garish for the room and its other furnishings.

High-gloss finishes are durable and easy to wipe clean, but then reflect light and can be annoying to live with. Semigloss and satin finishes are easier on the eyes and are just as satisfactory for the projects here.

Of course, before you apply brush to wood, there is sanding and filling to do. Lots of it. Storage projects, utilitarian though they are, need almost as much preliminary work as fine furniture simply because they get plenty of use—and abuse.

SANDING, FILLING, AND SEALING

Lumber should get a rough preliminary sanding with 80-grit paper to prepare the wood for handling and to point up any dents or gouges that need to be filled.

For filler, use wood putty, ready-mixed wallboard compound, plastic wood paste, or a vinyl spackling compound if you plan to paint.

For stains and clear finishes, use a filler of wood putty mixed with water-soluble color that will match the wood.

After fillers are applied, sand with 120-grit paper. Dust with tack cloth and final sand with 180-grit paper. Dust again with tack cloth and seal with one of the clear lacquer sanding sealers. Let dry for twenty-four hours and handsand again, lightly, with superfine grit.

If you plan to use a clear polyurethane varnish as a final finish, use the urethane itself as the sealer and give the surface several coats, fine-sanding between each one. The polyurethanes can go on over stains but don't mingle too well with the chemistry of ordinary shellac or the lacquer sanding sealers.

If the wood is to be stained, use a type you like and trust: alcohol-based stains, penetrating oil stains, or a pigmented wiping stain.

If the wood is to be stained, use a type you like and trust: polyurethanes, seal the wood with two coats of clear shellac—sanding between coats—and add one or more coats of ordinary varnish, fine-sanding between each application.

Primers for paint, which will be enamel, should be one of the enamel undercoatings applied with a brush. When dry, sand lightly by hand and brush on, or spray on, the enamel of your choice. Plan to give storage projects two coats of enamel (for more durable finish) and sand lightly between each application with wet-and-dry paper, working it in a pool of water to prevent scratching.

Softwood plywood will not need rough sanding; the manufacturer has already done that. Give the surface a preliminary sanding with 120-grit paper. Fill and treat holes and blemishes in the same manner as stock lumber.

Final-sand with 180-grit paper and dust thoroughly with a tack cloth. If you're going to paint, use a penetrating sealer like Firzite as an undercoat. When the undercoat is dry, sand again lightly by hand, dust well with the tack cloth, and paint. Rub down the first coat of paint with fine steel wool, clean with tack cloth, and apply final coat of paint.

Natural finishes on softwood plywood are not as visually exciting as those on hardwood plywood because the latter have finer, more interesting grain patterns. However, there are bound to be projects of softwood plywood that need not be painted; so a clear finish makes good sense. Use polyurethane varnish as both sealer and final coating.

Hardwood plywood, though more expensive than the softwood, assures a better natural finish with less effort. If you've planned all along to have a clear finish, select a good quality material with face veneer (and back, if needed) that most resembles the final wood tone you want. Fill holes and marks according to your favorite method, then sand with fine grit paper, dust, and sand again with a superfine grit, dusting with tack cloth each time. Apply the clear finish you prefer: shellac under varnish, or else a polyurethane.

Fir-veneered plywood is the least expensive and most widely used material for storage projects. Its face veneer, however, is a complex combination of high, swooping ridges, low valleys, plus dense and porous grains that play havoc with paints and stains. Sand it forever, and the ridges still defy leveling.

Choose fir veneered plywood only for projects whose appearance is not crucial. Bypass stains, they will only streak anyway, and give the wood a clear finish with shellac and varnish, or with a polyurethane varnish.

Painting fir plywood calls for a bit more effort to prepare the surface, but the final results can be pleasing. And the money you save in buying the material can be worth the extra work it takes to make it attractive. The procedure is this:

After the material is cut in all the shapes and sizes required by the project, sand with 120-grit paper just to smooth any glaring roughness on face and edges.

Dampen the surface (that will show) with a moist cloth or sponge. Slather vinyl spackling compound over all surfaces and edges, using a broad flexible blade. Immediately scrape off excess by drawing a wide, straight-edged scrap of wood across the surface and the edges. This will expose the ridges but leave the valleys filled in.

When the spackle is dry, sand with medium and fine grits, dusting thoroughly between each sanding. Then brush on an undercoat for the paint. When the undercoat is dry, sand again until the surfaces feel dry and smooth, not porous or gritty. Dust well with a damp, then dry cloth and apply paint.

COVERING PLYWOOD EDGES. Unless filled in or completely covered, plywood edges always look rough and unfinished; they detract from the overall appearance of shelves and cabinets. But there are a number of ways to make these edges presentable.

The spackle method. Fill and cover the raw edges with vinyl spackling compound. Work spackle into the ply edges with a narrow flexible blade; scrape off excess and let dry. Repeat the process once or twice more, or until the dry, treated edge will cause a drop of water to bead on its surface.

Once plywood edges are filled and closed by this method, you can cover them with paint, or with one of the pressure-sensitive plastic tapes. These tapes come in a variety of widths, and almost any color you can want, including bright mirror-like silvery mylar.

Wood veneer tapes give the most ordinary plywood the finished look of fine hand-rubbed hardwood. These tapes come in rolls of varied widths and are strong, flexible bands of real wood. Almost every variety of fine wood is represented so you can select one that matches face veneer on the plywood. Or you can create an interesting effect—for example, by banding the edges of white-painted shelves with rich teak veneer tape. Wood veneer tapes come with peel-and-stick adhesive backings, heat sensitive adhesive backings, or the kind that must be applied with white glue or contact cement.

For proper adhesion, edges of the plywood should be as firm, straight, smooth and free of dust as you can manage. If you use one of the pressure-sensitive wood veneer tapes, strip off a little of its paper backing a bit at a time as you work, to keep the adhesive from making contact before you are ready.

Use this same technique as you begin to apply heat-sensitive wood veneer tapes. The tape will hold as you hand-press it into position, but to create a permanent bond, iron it with a household iron at a temperature setting recommended for cotton. You'll use dry heat, not steam.

Though it takes practice and a steady hand, tapes applied with contact cement hold fast and achieve an exceptionally strong bond. Certain projects in highly visible locations will warrant this much attention. To apply contact cement, use a narrow animal-bristle brush and coat both the tape and the plywood edge with a thin, even layer of contact cement. Let the cement dry. Give the plywood edge a second coat, and let it dry. (The first coat will have soaked into the blotter-like raw edge.) Contact cement bonds immediately to itself upon contact, so there is no way to correct alignment of the tape as you lay it along the raw edge. It will help, though, if you slip a piece of newspaper or aluminum foil between the two cement-coated surfaces and slide it along ahead of you as you tape small sections at a time. The cement will not adhere to the paper or foil. When all the edges are taped, roll them with a rolling pin, seam roller, or length of wood dowel to remove air pockets and assure a firm all-over grip.

If you use white glue, coat the tape once and the plywood edge twice with an even layer of adhesive. Let the glue become tacky before setting the tape into position.

To final-finish wood veneer tape, trim away excess at corners or overhangs with a single-edge razor blade. Then lightly sand the edges of the veneer (but not its surface) to create a subtle merging of tape with plywood surface.

Wood strips and moldings, glue-nailed to raw plywood edges, give added dimension to a shelf or cabinet. They can also make a plywood slab look thicker—a worthwhile illusion for economical 1/2-inch plywood shelving, for example, which is strong enough to hold books but tends to look thin and weak in long expanses.

Strips should be glue-nailed into place, and clamped until dry. A straight piece of scrap wood between strip and clamp will help distribute pressure along the edge being covered.

Shaped or straight moldings glue-nailed to plywood edges give different styling effects—period or contemporary—to shelves and cabinets.

If cut a certain way, the plywood can act as its own cover. A rabbet cut in one plywood edge that leaves the last ply intact makes a perfect cover-up for the second joining plywood edge.

3 | Hardware and Moldings

ORNAMENTAL EMBELLISHMENT has an important place in any discussion about storage. Even though we tend to think of cabinets, shelves, and closets as mainly utilitarian, there are situations where plain, unadorned structures would look as out of place as a hacksaw on a coffee table.

Unless your project is intended for basement, attic, or garage, chances are it will need some decorative detailing to bring it into harmony with the surroundings—Colonial, Oriental, Early American, Contemporary. There are many ways you can use decorative moldings and hardware, papers and fabrics to endow it with the style you want.

Deftly applied, richly carved strips of wood bestow special distinction on structures that originally had no style at all.

Masses of decorative metal hardware on a cabinet creates extraordinary impact. Use Oriental style-coordinated groups of pulls, knobs, corner covers, latch plates, and hinges. For fullest effect, don't hesitate to pile it on, even though a natural tendency has always been to install simple knobs and hinges and nothing more.

Drawer pulls, door pulls, knobs, escutcheons, and cabinet ornaments are available in so many styles and materials it is impossible to show them all.

Decorative metal grilles give inexpensive insert-panels and larger open-panel doors rich, new dimension.

Open cane webbing, applied with white glue or staples, endows ordinary flush and paneled doors with new texture and style. Try it on closet and cabinet doors. On drawer fronts, too. Cover cut webbing edges with strips of wood molding. Webbing can be painted or left natural.

Porcelain doorknobs dress up closets and other room-size storage structures; the Three-In-One room divider in Chapter 14, for instance.

WOOD MOLDINGS. Carved and shaped wood strips also lend structural embellishment to shelves, cabinets, closets, large storage enclosures. Here again, plain unadorned surfaces can be

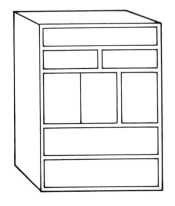

Massed hardware effects can be successful if materials and style are compatible. Plain and fancy Oriental trims in brass can create decorative impact on a chest that is to be painted in appropriate colors.

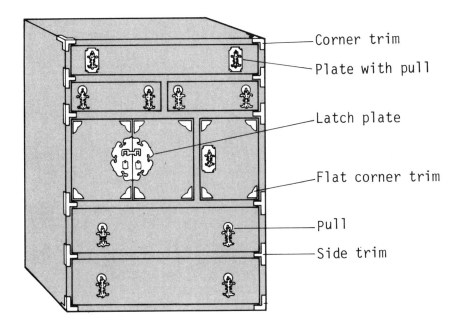

Corner trim

Plate with pull

Latch plate

Flat corner trim

Pull

Side trim

transformed into period-style pieces with moldings, a coping saw or miter box, and small brads.

Crown molding changed the look and proportion of the concealed bed storage-shell in Chapter 15. Without it, the cabinet would look too angular, and unfinished.

Cutting such large moldings requires a miter box, since lengths must rest in the box in the same position they will be installed. Outside cornering, such as on the storage shell, is done by making 45° cuts on an outward angle.

Hundreds of drawer pulls, door pulls, knobs, escutcheons, cabinent ornaments are available in decorative hardware shops. These are only a few of the styles you can use to make ordinary projects look extraordinary.

Open cane webbing can be surface-mounted with white glue or staples. Cover cut edges with molding strips. Paint, leave natural, or coat with clear polyurethane varnish.

You can make a separate lift-off crown molding cap for a structure that needs extra height or is due for a style-change.

Surface-mounted strips of molding give cabinets and shelf edges style and texture. All such applications look better—and professional—if they are mitered rather than butt-jointed at corners. To avoid splitting narrow strips, drill holes for brads, and drive last hits with a nail-set to avoid hammer marks on the surface of the molding. Countersink brads and fill holes with wood filler before final finishing.

There are hundreds of molding styles and sizes for decorative applications. Many are readily available in home centers and lumberyards. Others may have to be special-ordered by your dealer but are worth waiting for if you want a project to be distinctive.

In addition to these ornamental moldings, there are the less elaborate ones used for trim around door frames, on baseboards, at ceiling and wall junctures, outside corners. Profiles of some of the moldings most often stocked by lumber and building supply dealers are shown on pages 26 and 27. Their basic purpose, of course, is to impart a finished look to any project, whatever its size or location. Browse through the stock bin at your dealer's,

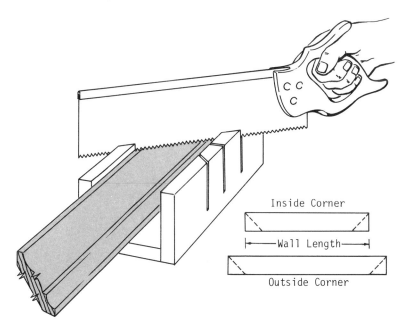

Crown molding should be cut in a miter box. Diagram shows how to measure length of molding for inside and outside corners.

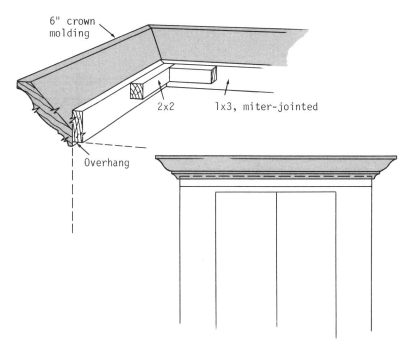

A removable crown-cap can be made by attaching the crown molding to a braced frame. Completed cap slips onto existing structure that needs more height or a fast style-change.

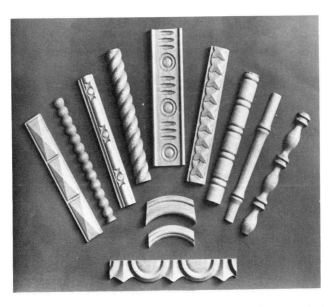

Hardwood moldings are ready to apply with brads or adhesive. These are just a few of the many sizes and forms available at hardware stores. *Courtesy Klise Manufacturing Co.*

Bamboo molding was used to change a stark, modern cabinet into one with a more traditional decor.

Intricate formations of embossed wood are massed on a cabinet to give it a new look. Ornaments of this delicacy need to be framed by moldings to keep them from looking lost on large expanses.

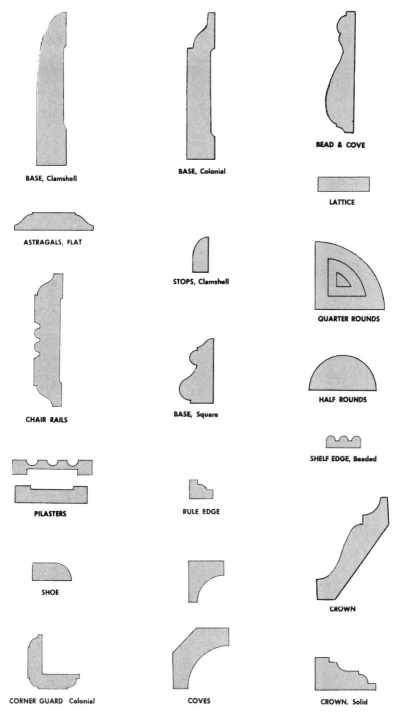

BASE, Clamshell

BASE, Colonial

BEAD & COVE

LATTICE

ASTRAGALS, FLAT

STOPS, Clamshell

QUARTER ROUNDS

CHAIR RAILS

BASE, Square

HALF ROUNDS

SHELF EDGE, Beaded

PILASTERS

RULE EDGE

SHOE

CROWN

CORNER GUARD Colonial

COVES

CROWN, Solid

Some of the more basic and often used moldings that are available at lumberyards, home centers, some hardware stores.

look over his charts of available styles and sizes, and plan in advance which moldings will best suit the style and finished appearance of a given project.

Embossed wood ornaments glued to plain surfaces create a look of intricate panel-carving. They are lightweight and delicate; apply them with glue. Mass them in close groupings within borders of molding, otherwise they will look as though cast adrift on a blank sea of wood.

PAPER AND FABRIC ACCENTS. Closets, cabinets, drawers, bookcases, cubes, and wall-hung boxes can be made colorfully interesting with panels and linings of paper, fabric, cork, even leather. Often most such coverings can be held in place on walls and backings with double-faced tape or staples. Staples can be concealed with cloth tape or molding strips.

To glue coverings into place, choose an adhesive best suited to the material being installed, and properly prepare the surface being covered. Follow these guidelines:

To glue fabric or paper to new wood, sand the backing and add a primer undercoat. When dry, brush on a coating of white glue thinned with water (half-and-half). While glue is still wet, smooth cut-to-size paper or fabric into place.

To glue fabric or paper to old plaster, wallpaper, or paint, scrape all loose patches off the surface. Prime with wallpaper size or one of the resin sealers. Coat the surface with white glue-and-water

China cabinet with buffet serving counter was built into an old closet. Patterned vinyl wallcovering is used to line shelves and wall behind shelves and define drawers and cabinet doors. *Courtesy Comark Plastics Division.*

Linen closet is fully lined in a small patterned wallcovering that match panels on doors and vanity cabinet drawers. *Comark Plastics Division.*

mixture or one of the wall covering adhesives listed in the chart on page 30.

To apply decorative coverings to glossy paint surface, de-gloss with a detergent floor-cleaning product; size, and install covering with appropriate adhesive.

Cork, if backed with paper, can be applied with wheat paste. If the backing material is burlap, use vinyl wall-covering adhesive.

To apply leather (cowhide), use mildew resistant vinyl wall covering compound. When dry, clean and polish the leather with a paste floor wax.

To apply suede or suede-cloth, use staples. Cover staples with borders of piping or molding strips.

Paper and vinyl wallcoverings can endow even the simplest storage structures with style and visual impact. They give texture and pattern to surfaces that often look too plain, too boring. Linen closets, china and glassware cabinets especially, look better with some color on the back walls or shelves.

The dining room closet in the photo opposite (left), for example, is lined with prepasted, strippable wall covering, giving warmth to a space that would look cold, too sleek, in an otherwise warmly furnished room.

The photo opposite (right) shows a linen closet fully lined inside, and covered on the outside, with small patterned vinyl. Unless shelves can be removed, cover the back wall with cut-to-size sections of the wallcovering. Then wrap each shelf separately; that is, cover the shelf full with one length of the prepasted vinyl covering. For door panels, cut sections that will fit between the molding trim. Even dark kitchen cabinets can be enlivened with simple inserts of wallcovering cut to fit within molding border. To cover drawer fronts, remove pulls, press prepasted sections of the vinyl covering into place, reattach pulls to drawer.

Whole wall systems can be up-dated or given a new decorative scheme when covered in a check-patterned Con-Tact Brand A-1 Adhesive. The adhesive formulation allows the covering to be shifted or repositioned before adhesive sets. Note that walls are painted to match dominant color in the checked covering.

To cover a wall, or any surface, with fabric you can use the glues and adhesives outline in the chart on page 30, or use heavy-duty double-faced tape, or you can use staples. Stapling is especially recommended if you're installing thick or quilted materials. You can use one of two fastening methods. If you have a small amount of wall surface to cover, staple furring strips of thin lattice or lath strips to the wall at top, bottom, and where side seams or joints

Dark kitchen cabinets can be enlivened with wallcovering inserts of the same pattern as surrounding walls. *Comark Plastics Division.*

Check-patterned Con-Tact Brand A-1 Adhesive vinyl covers a wall system, giving it a fresh look but more important, making it easy to wipe clean. *Comark Plastics Division.*

will be. Staple fabric to the strips, starting at the top first. Then, stretching the fabric gently yet firmly, staple to the bottom furring strip. Stretch-and-staple one side of the fabric panel, then the other, to furring strips. If staples need to be covered, glue on fabric braid or self-welting.

Another method is to staple the fabric to sections of prefinished wall paneling, or to other thin but stiff material. This method is helpful when you have a large section of wall to cover. When the panels are all covered you can attach them to the walls with an electric staple gun capable of driving paneling nails.

GLUES AND ADHESIVES FOR PAPERS AND FABRICS

MATERIAL	ADHESIVE
Uncoated paper	Wheat paste
Vinyl-coated paper	Stainless cellulose paste
Vinyl, Foils or Flocked wall coverings	Mildew resistant vinyl compound
Pre-pasted wallpaper	(Water)
Grass cloth, burlap wall coverings	Wheat paste or cellulose paste (stainless)

4 | Shelves

SHELVES CAN be the fastest, easiest of all storage systems to build. They can also be exasperating and tricky to install. It all depends on the kinds of supports used and the composition of the wall on which the supports are to be fastened.

SHELF SYSTEMS. The simplest shelf arrangements are those you make by setting lengths of stock lumber across bricks, concrete or glass blocks, flue tile, or chunky wood posts. No tools. No fasteners. No problems. Existing wall and floor are adequate stabilizers provided you don't build the stack too high. A good general rule for maximum heights of arrangements like these is:

- Narrow shelves, 8 inches or less, not over 4 feet.
- Medium-wide shelves, 9 to 11 inches, not over 5 feet.
- Extra-wide shelves (of plywood slabs) 12 inches or more, not over 3 feet. (They're more likely to tip if load is pulled toward front edge.)

However, a combination of widths arranged setback fashion can be taken as high as 6 feet. Stacks anchored to the wall with L-brackets and appropriate fasteners can be built as high as you want.

Shaped spindles for shelf supports are available at home centers and building supply outlets. The spindles are predrilled for fastening to ready-made shelving or stock lumber. Size, shape, and arrangement possibilities for these systems are almost endless. The only restriction is height: the units will sway if built up too high. They should be either cross-braced at the back or anchored to the wall with L-brackets. But you can create a full-wall look simply by hanging two or more groupings on the wall over several low, floor-standing assemblies.

Another simplified shelf system is possible with manufactured heavy-duty metal tension poles slotted to take adjustable brackets. These can hold very heavy loads, such as records, books, large cans of paint. The tension poles are expensive but worth the price because they are dependably strong and easy to install.

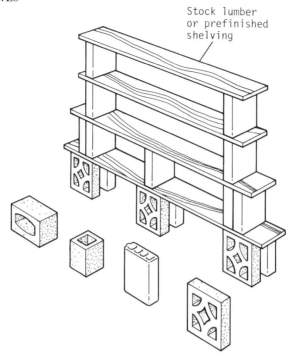

Stock lumber
or prefinished
shelving

Instant shelf systems are made with stock lumber or prefinished shelving set across ready-made bricks, cement blocks, and the like. Where blocks and boards rest against wall or floor, add glued-on strips of felt or cork.

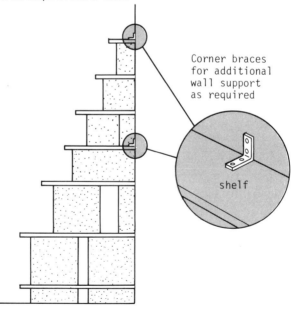

Corner braces
for additional
wall support
as required

shelf

Arranged as set-back, unanchored block and board shelves can be stacked as high as six feet. Higher stacks need fastening however. Anchor several shelves to wall with L-brackets fastened to their back edge; see Detail above.

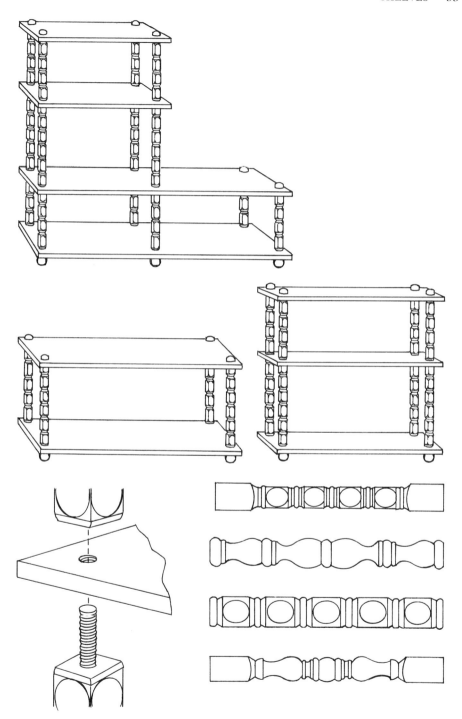

Size and shape arrangement possibilities are many with a system of boards and shaped spindles and posts. Floor units, together with wall-hung shelves, create a total-wall effect.

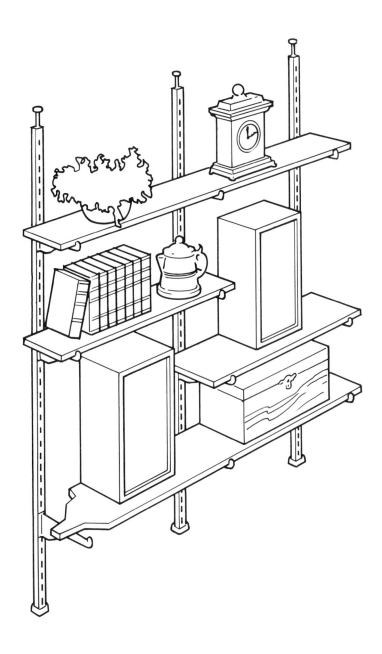

Heavy-duty slotted tension poles can hold heavy loads on shelves held in place by adjustable metal brackets. Poles are available at shelf shops and some hardware stores.

Floating
shelf

Bore hole to beyond
center of shelf

Iron
rod

Wall
stud

Floating, or cantilevered, shelves must be made of at least 2-inch nominal stock. Accurate drilling is necessary to assure true alignment between iron rods and wall studs. Make holes slightly smaller than diameter of the rod. Tap rods into studs. Tap shelf onto rods by striking front edge with mallet or hammer buffered by a piece of scrap.

Floating shelves are dramatic because they have no visible means of support; no hardware shows at all. Yet they are strong, serviceable, and relatively easy to install. Matching holes are driven into wall studs and the back edge of the shelf. Iron rods in the holes secure the shelf to the wall.

Cleats of scrap wood, quarter-round or shaped moldings nailed and glued to uprights are the most economical shelf supports you can make. They are not aesthetically pleasing for all installations but are first-rate and functional for inside closets, pantry, utility cabinets, on basement and garage walls, in attics. Cleats used in cabinets and systems open to view are best covered up with face-trimming or molding strips, otherwise the primary structure will look pieced-together. Other supports include dowels, flanged metal pegs, L-shaped hooks—almost anything that can be pushed into pre-drilled holes or driven into a set of uprights. The accompanying drawing shows some of the most common supports of this type.

Triangular shelf supports of curved metal or carved wood make the plainest slab of wood look rich. If you are lucky enough to find a couple of matching Victorian porch-roof corner braces, use them. No matter how beat-up or gouged, they will look properly important when sanded and painted.

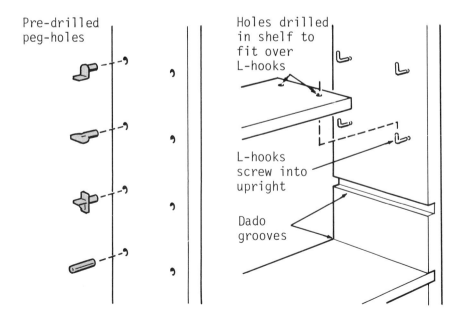

Pre-drilled peg-holes

Holes drilled in shelf to fit over L-hooks

L-hooks screw into upright

Dado grooves

A few of the many easy ways to support shelves between two uprights.

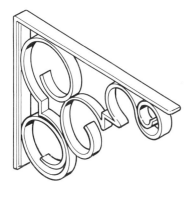 

Two of many interesting triangular shelf supports that you can buy, make, or be lucky enough to find at auctions, demolition sites, salvage yards. At left, a curved metal shelf support; at right, a recycled Victorian porch corner brace.

Shelves fitted into dado-grooved uprights not only reflect good craftsmanship but contribute considerably to the dimensional stability of the structure itself.

Shelf standards of slotted metal strips look simple enough—until you begin installing them. You must make sure the wall material is strong enough to support the expected loaded weight of the shelf. If that's questionable, fasten the standards directly into wall studs with long wood screws. If because of the arrangement the standards cannot be attached to studs, use the kind of fastener best suited to the wall material.

Have an assortment of fasteners on hand before you begin: for masonry, wallboard, plaster (thick and thin)—all can be used in installing these standards for a full-wall system of shelves. There is one inescapable advantage to shelf supports of this kind. The shelves can be moved up, down, or removed any time you want to adjust them. Such versatility is often worth the extra effort that's needed to install a system properly.

Wooden standards are an improvement over bare metal ones. The wood can be trimmed and finished to blend with a room's style and furnishings. Being wider, the support-strip can be easier to handle than long narrow ones. Ready-made standards are available in shelf shops and many hardware stores and come in various styles and finishes. Or, you can make them yourself out of stock lumber, as shown in the accompanying drawing on page 39.

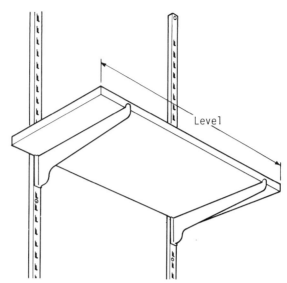

Mount shelf standards on wall with the aid of a piece of scrap lumber and spirit level. First, mount one standard and install a bracket. Then hold the second standard, with a bracket installed, against the wall. Using scrap (to simulate a shelf) and level, adjust the standard so the two brackets align. Also use level to be sure standards are vertical.

SHELVING MATERIAL. Almost anything that's flat and capable of spanning a space can be used for shelving: slate, marble, fine hardwood, inexpensive lumber, plywood, glass, clear and colored plastics, man-made marble, flush doors, old doors, shutters. Just choose shelving according to the look you want, and the weight it will carry.

Tradition has decreed, for some reason, that a shelf-span of wood should be supported every 30 inches. But since wall studs are spaced on 16-inch centers, and studs are easier to fasten into than wall material alone, why not go the extra 2 inches for a 32-inch span over every other stud? Such a method will greatly simplify most installations.

Wooden shelves look better if they are $^3/_4$-inch or more in thickness. Half-inch plywood has as much support-power as an equal length of pine stock, for example, but it looks skimpy. You can use the thinner material (and save money) in systems where function rather than appearance is important.

A truly worthwhile shelf system is more than rows of equally spaced boards. The distance between horizontals should accommodate the size and shape of the things being stored. There should be knuckle space between the tops of books and the shelf

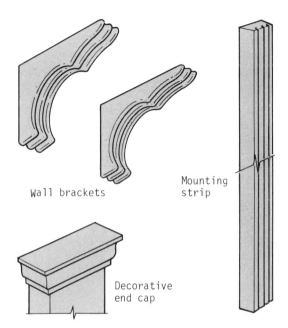

Wall brackets

Mounting strip

Decorative end cap

Ready-made mounting strips are available in stores, home centers, shelf shops. They come with matching brackets and can have decorative end caps.

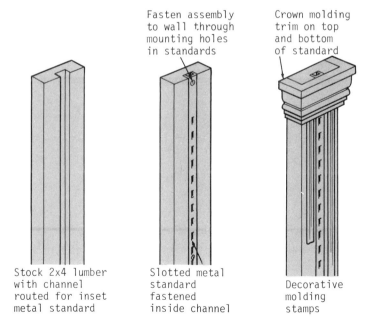

Fasten assembly to wall through mounting holes in standards

Crown molding trim on top and bottom of standard

Stock 2x4 lumber with channel routed for inset metal standard

Slotted metal standard fastened inside channel

Decorative molding stamps

Make your own wood mounting strips and finish with caps and vertical molding strips. Paint to match shelf color.

above. Some shelves should be wider than others so that objects can be safely stored but easily reached. Narrow objects need narrow shelves, otherwise they will become jumbled. Small drawers under shelves increase storage space and extend the uses of the shelf system. Set small or medium-sized cabinets on shelves within a system and you create still more uses for the total arrangement; cabinets can hold toys, china, glassware, barware, sweaters. You will see in later chapters how shelves, combined with cabinets, even closets, create storage structures having even more versatility.

5 | Case Making

ENCLOSED STORAGE has many sizes and forms. A cube is the smallest unit, a closet the largest. In between these are cabinets which are as capable of adapting to space requirements as shelves are.

The framing techniques you use to create a cabinet will be determined in large part by the material you use, the purpose the case is to serve, and by the money you want to spend on the project.

An assembly of wood slabs forms a case frame. An assembly of rails also forms a case frame.

Use slab framing when the material is thick enough and strong enough to allow the case parts to be joined securely to each other. Many storage projects here are slab constructed—large roll-out bins, a swing-out pantry, a wall of boxes. Other projects require box framing—where economy, as well as greater load-strength and stability, are the main concerns.

In general, slab framing is more expensive than box framing because of the thick material used. Box frames, on the other hand, are made of lesser grade stock lumber and can be covered with thinner, often less costly, material.

MAKING BOX FRAMES. The two construction methods shown on the following pages are exceptionally well suited for building storage cabinets. In the lap- and butt-jointed assembly two lap-jointed rectangles, or squares for that matter, with four uprights butt-joined to them, form the basic framework. A long cabinet will need a mid-lap brace across top and bottom members, as shown on page 42, but this can be omitted on shorter spans.

Fully butt-jointed frames are faster to build, and often are just as sturdy as lap-jointed ones. The frame shown on page 43 can be made of 2x2s or larger stock sizes. For long expanses, several such frames set side-by-side present one distinct advantage: solid frames from which to hang doors are there, ready and waiting. Obviously, a lot of material is used in an assembly of this kind, but since extra framing and bracing are not needed, the cost evens itself out in the long run.

Turning a box frame into a cabinet is now a matter of fastening an outer covering to the frame, installing shelves and doors. Fasten the enclosed case to a recessed base of 2x4s laid on edge and you have adequate toe-space without having to notch side panels or install a kickplate.

The basic box frame does not always have to be enclosed, however. It is by itself, a versatile form whose very openness offers certain advantages—storage that's well ventilated, easy to reach, easy to arrange. It houses not only pull-out sorting bins, which are ordinary plastic wastebaskets, but allows hooks, pegs, and rods to be placed wherever they are handiest for the person using them.

Consider the useful possibilities of a tall, open box frame set on end. It becomes a closet for hanging rainwear and sports clothing that need ventilated drying space. Here, the unit is composed of end-lapped 2x3s supported and connected by 1¼-inch dowels which are also the hanging rods and ventilated shelves for rainhats, wet boots.

A closet such as this has many practical advantages in ski and beach cottages as well as primary homes. A rubberized drip-tray slides under the dowel base to catch runoff from footwear and

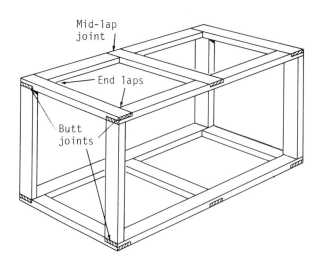

Basic box frame with lap and butt joints. A long box frame needs a mid-lap joint to support the center.

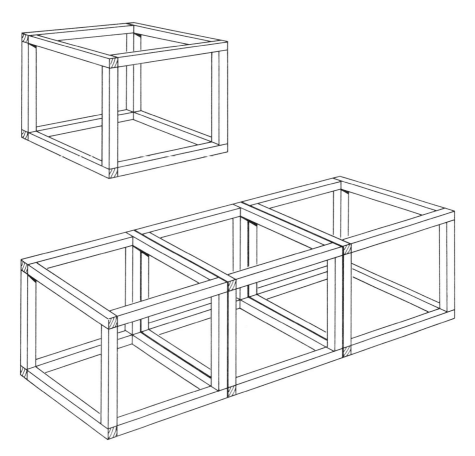

Butt-jointed box frame, Top and bottom sections are butted and joined in clockwise fashion. Several butt-joined box frames create a long frame.

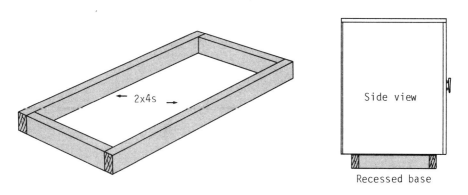

Recessed base made of 2x4s on edge and butt-joined automatically forms a $3\frac{1}{2}$-inch toe
space under a case.

clothing. The finish can be a clear, natural one or bright enamel in several different colors.

Apply the same principle to create an etagere for books, plants, and stereo equipment. The unit is as tall and as wide as the closet but less deep: 14 inches front to back. Add dowels across the front to support shelves of tempered glass, plastic, or wood.

Still another version of the open box frame is a waist-high unit that slopes upward, about 20 degrees, toward the back. It can be used to hold tablecloths, napkins, placemats in wrinkle-free condition. Blankets, sheets, pillowcases also are easier to store on a rack such as this rather than in stacks on shelves or in drawers. Dimensions of the frame should be determined by the space in which the unit will be placed—closet or laundry room, for instance—and by personal preference as to height, width, slope.

Slope of the frame allows for longer items to be hung over dowels in the back. However, since the slope would complicate end-lap joining, the 2x3s are surface joined with glue, nails or screws, and dowels. Squared ends at top corners of the frame are sawed off to conform to the angle of slope. Sand the rack

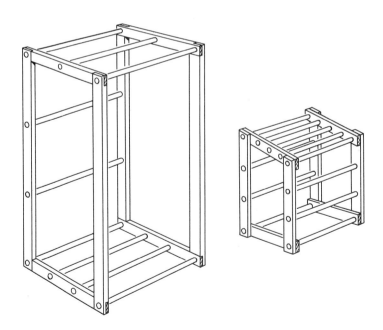

Tall, open box frame (left) of end-lapped 2x3s serves as a closet for hanging rainwear and sports clothing that need ventilated drying space. Waist-high unit (right) can be used to store tablecloths, napkins, placemats, bedclothes in wrinkle-free condition.

Full-wall storage system of ladders provides see-through storage and plenty of hanging space for clothing. This system is the basis for a garage wall shown in Chapter 17.

thoroughly, to eliminate snagging and binding, and give it a clear finish.

There is yet another use for the sloped box frame. Add casters and you will create a handy rolling rack for hanging things taken fresh from the dryer or ironing board.

Traditionally, full-wall storage systems consist of solid-panel shelves and uprights. But a new form with extended uses becomes possible when the horizontals and verticals are ladders instead of slabs. (See the garage wall-organizer in Chapter 17.) Being of ladders, the whole system is see-through (objects stored overhead are easy to find) and there are plenty of instantly ready places from which to hang things.

Depending upon the weight and size of the items being stored, ladders can be made of 1x2s, 2x2s, 2x3s, 2x4s, with dowel rods or not. Use any combination of stock sizes, and any kind of joint that best suits the job.

MAKING SLAB FRAMES. It takes time to cut rabbet and dado grooves into slabs but once that's done, final assembly moves along quickly. Moreover, the need for inner bracing is eliminated: once the component parts are fitted together, a cabinet made with these joints has superior strength and stability. Such joinery is especially suitable for plywood whose edges and ends do not hold nails and screws well.

Any combination of joints can be used for putting slab frames together. Side pieces can be rabbetted at one end to take a top, and dadoed at the other to hold the bottom shelf. Interior shelves can be dadoed into place, butt-jointed to cabinet sides, or set on adjustable supports. Or the whole cabinet can be butt-jointed together.

Although butt-jointed slab frames are easy to make, they need special bracing and fastenings to assure stability. Screws, for example, make a butt-joint more secure than nails do. Dowels make a stronger joint than screws. Glue-blocks, cleats, or L-brackets brace butt-jointed slabs from the inside.

CABINET BACKS. Backings can be of the same material used in the main body of the cabinet, or they can be made of thinner material such as luan, $1/2$- or $1/4$-inch plywood, $1/4$- or $1/8$-inch hardboard. Whatever is used it should be fastened with glue and nails, or screws, and filled with wood paste to close seams and gaps.

Backing can be fastened directly over the cabinet's back edges (inset $1/8$th of an inch all around) or slipped into dado grooves cut in the sides. They can also be set into the cabinet frame and

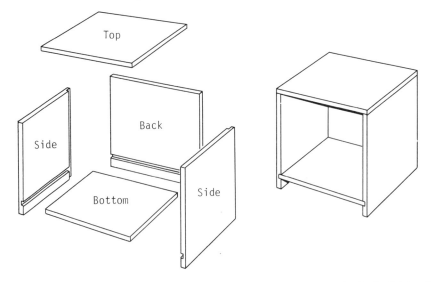

Butt-joined slab frame with sides dadoed for bottom. The bottom can also be butt-joined to the sides, but the dadoes provide added strength.

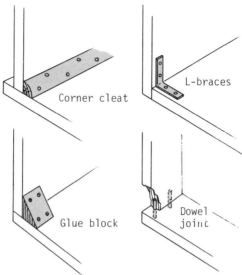

Four ways of reinforcing butt joints.

fastened to inside cleats. Thicker backing material, of $^3/_4$-inch or $^1/_2$-inch plywood, can be inset flush with the cabinet frame and nailed into place by driving nails through the outside of the cabinet into the edges of the backing.

For cabinet backs that will be visible, use the same material as the main body. If you plan to cover the back with decorative paper, fabric, or cork, a thinner material can be used. If a cabinet is to be wall-hung with fasteners through its backing, use $^1/_2$ inch or thicker material.

MAKING CUBES. Open five-sided cubes are ideal storage structures in that several of them grouped together form what is essentially a cabinet with compartments. Moreover, they can be arranged different ways at different times to serve a wide variety of storage functions, such as the attic storage tower in Chapter 18, and the variations illustrated on page 49.

The only point to keep in mind when building cubes is that, though by definition an open cube has five equal sides, the parts are anything but equal in size. This is because the thickness of the material has to be figured into the dimensions of each section. The trick to building cubes successfully is to think of its parts not as sides but as separate pieces with names: a top, a bottom, two sides, and a back. Now each section has meaning in terms of cutting and assembly. Then follow this little guide for figuring cutting dimensions:

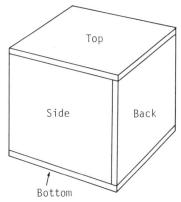

Method of constructing the basic cube. Note that sides are cut shorter than top and bottom to allow for inset back.

● Top and bottom are the only two sections having the finished dimensions of the cube.

● Sides fit between top and bottom so are rectangles.

● Back fits between sides as well as top and bottom, so is a smaller square.

Fasten storage cubes together with cream-colored glue and screws or nails, countersinking them. Material can be hardwood, plywood, stock lumber, plastic, or particleboard.

GETTING AROUND BASEBOARDS. Baseboards do not become a part of the storage-building process until it's time to install a cabinet, closet, or shelves. Then the need for giving them prior consideration is fully appreciated. At that point you have only two choices: settle for a gap between the structure and the wall or take out a portion of the baseboard.

To remove the baseboard, locate nearest seams and pry off the board and its molding trims if any. Set these aside. After the cabinet or closet is installed, cut and refit the baseboard up to the storage unit, or around it if the structure is a large one, such as a closet or built-in.

Considered *before* construction begins, the baseboard problem can be handled in a number of ways. They are: (1) Notch back edges of the side panels to fit over the baseboard. (2) Scribe the shape of the baseboard onto the side panels, and cut with a coping saw. (3) Install a recessed base high enough to raise the cabinet over the baseboard.

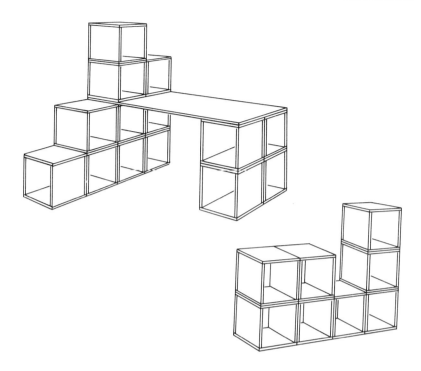

Cubes can be arranged in various ways to provide storage. Unit at top includes a desk.

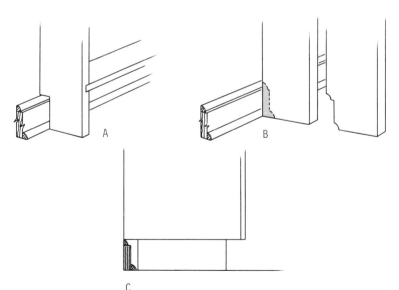

Three ways to get around baseboard: (A) notch the back edge of side panel; (B) scribe the shape of the baseboard onto the panel and cut with a coping saw; (C) Install a recessed base that raises the cabinet high enough to clear the baseboard.

6 | Cabinet Doors and Hinges

A SINGLE DOOR, double doors, or a row of doors give cabinets finish and character. Decide on the kind you want to install—sliding, hinged, or drop-down—at the time you plan and order material and hardware for your project.

Sliding doors. These are the simplest to make and install. They are also the most inexpensive in terms of material and hardware. Though sliding doors limit access to the contents of the cabinet, they are a wise choice for projects that will be installed in narrow spaces where swing-out door space is restricted. Another difficulty is that sliding doors impart a contemporary look to the cabinet in which they are used. There is nothing within the scope of decorative hardware or trims that can disguise this feature.

Material for sliding doors is varied—and widely available. Any flat, smooth, rigid $1/4$ inch or $1/2$ inch material makes good sliding doors. Glass, plastic, plywood, hardboard are most commonly used.

You can rout sliding door track grooves in the cabinet frame with a router, or create track-grooves with surface-mounted molding strips. Or you can buy lengths of ready-made grooved track for doors that are $1/8$ inch, $1/4$ inch or $1/2$ inch in thickness. Whether you make or buy grooved track, keep in mind that the top grooves should be $3/8$ inch deep and the bottom ones $3/16$ inch deep (or a comparable proportion) so the doors can be lifted up into the top and lowered down into the bottom. That done, installation is completed. Sand door edges and track grooves to assure smooth operation. Track grooves can be extended up the side of the cabinet if you want door edges concealed, or need to keep the interior free of dust and dirt.

Drop-down doors. These have the added distinction of being work surfaces when extended. For a flush fit, hinges must be mortised even with or slightly below both surfaces. Buy flush counter hinges or a continuous hinge and cut to length with a hacksaw. In using such a hinge, bevel the butting edges of the drop-down and

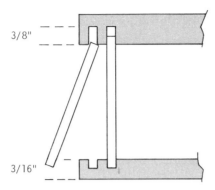

3/8"

3/16"

Routed track grooves for sliding doors.

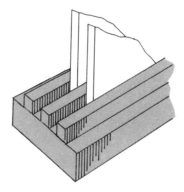

Make your own track grooves with surface-mounted wood strips. Glue-nail to cabinet top and bottom.

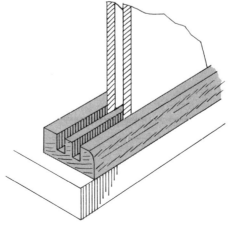

Ready-made track of wood, plastic, or metal. Fiber-lined track is available for glass and plastic doors at hardware and building supply stores.

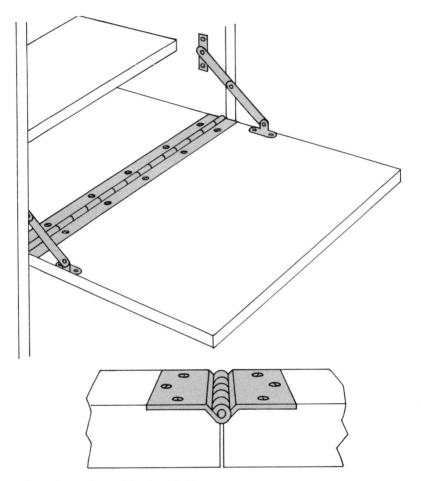

Drop-down door using continuous hinge.

its supporting shelf to hold the hinge's center ridge. Attach stay supports to the cabinet sides and to the surface of the drop-down.

Hinged doors. There are three basic types of doors you can make for cabinets—flush, lipped, or overlay. One door, the lipped, requires a rabbet cut along its hinged edge. The other two are plain slabs to which you attach certain kinds of hinges. There are two ways each door can be fitted to a cabinet—directly to its side, or to its face-frame.

Flush and overlay doors can be made of solid slabs that are $\frac{1}{2}$ inch to 1 inch in thickness, depending on how large the door has to be. Small doors $\frac{1}{2}$ inch thick are usually adequate for most storage cabinets. Large doors on large structures are best made of

$^3/_4$-inch, or thicker, material for both strength and appearance; a thin door on a sturdy frame looks out of proportion.

For proper fit, doors should be made $^1/_8$ inch less in size (all around) than the finished opening.

In general, doors on slab frame cabinets are made of the same material as the cabinet. Doors of solid lumber tend to warp unless made of narrow tongue-and-groove strips backed with a Z-brace.

The most popular material for cabinet doors is plywood. Hardwood plywood with lumber core is best, but others, if selected carefully for firmness, will usually serve well.

Lipped doors. There are two ways to make these. One is by cutting a rabbet into one edge; the other is to glue two panels together, the inside panel being smaller than the outer one. Use a strong-bonding adhesive. Weight or clamp the two pieces until the adhesive dries.

Three basic types of doors, the flush, overlay and lipped, can be installed in cabinets with or without a face frame.

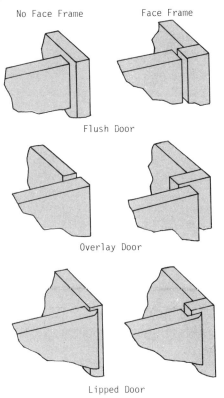

No Face Frame   Face Frame

Flush Door

Overlay Door

Lipped Door

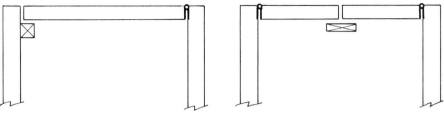

Stops for single and double flush doors.

HINGES. In choosing the kind of doors a cabinet will have, consider whether you want the hinges to be fully visible, partially visible, or completely concealed. Keep in mind also that some hinges must be mortised while others can be surface mounted. To what extent hinges will affect the cabinet's appearance is of secondary concern, because there are so many hinge designs you will have no trouble finding one that's right.

Butt hinges. For flush and overlay doors, these come in many shapes and sizes. They can be surface-mounted—and therefore are fully visible from the outside—or attached between the cabinet and door edge; only the pin portion of the hinge will show. This latter installation requires mortising. Use the hinge itself as a

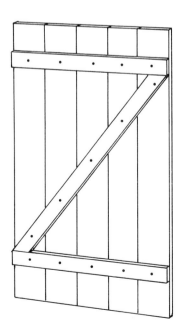

Solid lumber doors warp unless made of narrow strips, tongue-and-groove, and backed with a Z-brace.

template, then cut the mortise with a woodworking chisel and hammer or mallet. Loose-pin hinges are the easiest of this type to work with: the two leaves can be separated, installed individually and reassembled by putting the pin back into position.

How many hinges per door and how near top and bottom edges of the door should they be? A principle used by most builders is: If the door is longer than 2 feet, use three hinges, one in the center and the other two 4 inches from top and bottom edges. If two hinges are to be used, divide the length of the door into quarters, and place hinges on the top and bottom marks.

To determine what size hinges to use on doors over two feet long, measure the length of the door. Say it's 36 inches. Divide this by $\frac{1}{6}$; that's 6. Divide this by the number of hinges, three, and

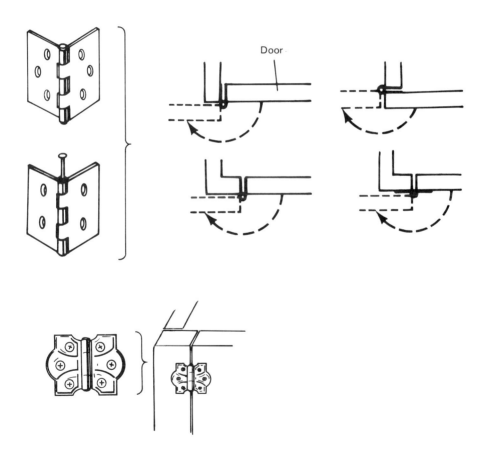

Butt hinges for flush and overlay doors.

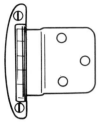 

Offset hinges for lipped and overlay doors.

you get 2. You need three 2-inch hinges. (Total length of hinges should be $^1/_6$ the length of the door.)

Offset hinges. For lipped and overlay doors these are available for surface mounting or for partially concealed installations. For lipped doors, the hinges' offset must match the size of the rabbet-edge in the door.

Pivot hinges. For both flush and overlay doors these are almost invisible from the outside; only the top of the pivot shows between cabinet and door edge. However, most pivot hinges require fastening into door edges, the weakest part of a plywood slab. If you choose pivot hinges, make the doors of lumber-core plywood if possible.

Concealed hinges. These can be used on flush and overlay doors. Most are expensive and tricky to install; they require deep mortising and precise alignment. Surface-mounted concealed hinges are easier to handle and though they are not widely available, they are being stocked by some specialty hardware stores.

KNOBS AND PULLS. These can be plain or fancy, but more important, they must be comfortable, easy to grip, and be selected for their ability to stand up under hard use.

Pivot hinges for flush and overlay doors.

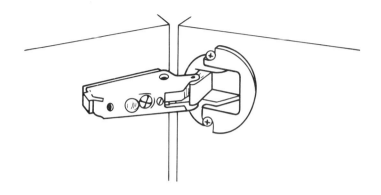

Concealed hinge for overlay doors.

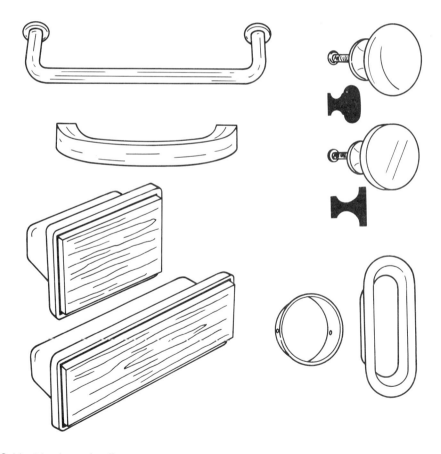

Cabinet knobs and pulls.

D-shaped handles are recommended for bins and large, heavy doors and drawers.

Bolt-on knobs are more durable than screw-in types and are available in many styles, sizes, and shapes.

Chunky, heavy knobs and pulls are strong, handsome additions to cabinets that will be used in living rooms, dens, hallways.

Recessed flush pulls of metal in round and oval shapes are for sliding doors. Select according to thickness of door.

Finger pulls for doors, drawers.

7 | Drawers

STORAGE DRAWERS must be strong in order to withstand frequent pulling and pushing. Drawer bottoms have to be sturdy enough not to give way under heavy weights, and firm enough to keep the drawer square. Sides and back have to stay rigid otherwise the drawer will not slide properly. Yet despite all this, you want the drawer to be as lightweight as possible.

Material for drawers, therefore, should be selected with care. Three-quarter-inch stock pine or fir would, at first glance, appear to be ideal for fronts, backs, and sides. Particularly if the sides are to be grooved for sliding on rails inside the cabinet. However, stock lumber, unless clear, dry, and very expensive, is likely to warp, causing more problems than you'd care to have.

The best bet, of course, is plywood. It is warp resistant and comes in a variety of thicknesses. If the drawer sides are to be grooved for rails, use $1/2$- to $5/8$-inch plywood. Most drawer bottoms can be of $1/4$-inch hardboard; it won't warp or sag out of shape. If drawers are to be used for storing very heavy things, then bottoms should be of $1/2$-inch or even $3/4$-inch plywood. Drawer bottoms of $1/4$-inch plywood are suitable unless hard-edged objects like tools or cans of paint are being stored.

For small drawers up to 14 inches wide use $3/8$-inch ply for sides and back, and $1/2$-inch for fronts.

Drawers from 14 to 30 inches wide need $1/2$-inch plywood sides and backs, and $3/4$-inch fronts. If the drawers are over 30 inches wide, and are designed to hold heavy things, use $1/2$-inch plywood for sides and back and $3/4$-inch material for fronts. Also, reinforce the drawer inside with quarter-round molding strips at corners and along bottom seams.

As a rule, the plywood you select for drawer sides should have good face veneers on both sides to assure a snag-free interior, and smooth operation when installed. But you can use a plywood with one good side (for the outside) if the drawer will be lined with paper, fabric, or thin sheet plastic.

Drawer fronts can be made of stock lumber as well as plywood,

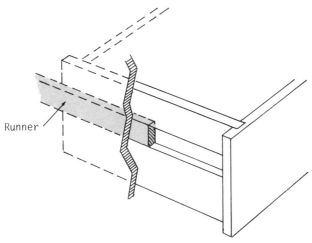

Attach drawer runners (of hardwood, if possible) to inside of cabinet with glue and wood screws. Cut dadoes in drawer sides.

especially if you plan to paint or give the cabinet a natural finish. But if you plan to cover the drawer front with plastic sheet or laminate, prefinished paneling, decorative papers or fabric, then use particleboard as a base. It's economical enough to allow you to splurge a little on the cover-up material.

Rails and runners. Of the many ways you can prepare drawers and

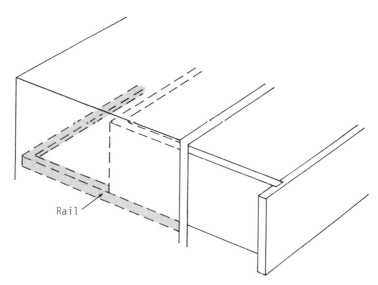

Attach rails to cabinet sides. Bottom edges of drawer and inside cabinet rails have to be sanded extra-smooth. Soap along drawer edges will help greatly.

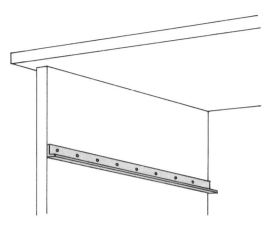

Metal drawer runners attached to cabinet sides. These must be properly aligned. Use level to check that runners on one side are even with those on the opposite side.

cabinets for slide-out storage, there are four that work well in slab and box frame constructions.

(1) Drawer sides are grooved to slide on runners fastened to the inside of the cabinet. By hook or crook, try to find hardwood for these runners. Once sanded smooth, they'll give trouble-free service for years.

(2) Drawer slides between supports rails (or slabs) inside the cabinet. Make sure all contact surfaces on both the drawer and rails are sanded very smooth.

(3) Drawer slides on L-shaped metal strips attached to cabinet sides. This represents one of the simplest ways to hold a drawer in place. However, once the strips are in place on one side, use ruler and level patiently and often to be sure the supports are in proper alignment.

(4) Drawer slides on metal extension glides fitted to both the drawer and cabinet sides. Installing extension glides also takes patience, careful measuring, and constant use of the level, especially if there is to be a series of glide-out drawers in one cabinet.

The secret to overall alignment and smooth operation is in avoiding the temptation to final-drive all screws the first time around. Instead, drive fasteners into the slotted openings you'll find in all the glide tracks. (There are also round screw-holes in the metal tracks, but wait; they're for later.) Slotted holes allow for a certain amount of preliminary adjustment as you put glide tracks and drawers through a test run. Then, if glide extension, align-

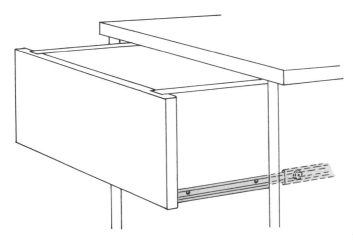

Metal extension glides. It takes patience and careful measuring to install them. Always have complete sets on hand *before* making drawers to be sure you leave enough space between sides of cabinet and drawer.

ment, and drawer operation are to your satisfaction, disassemble tracks and final drive all screws in the round holes.

Types of drawers. Four types of drawers are well suited to storage installations, and each is relatively simple to make.

(1) Rabbeted and dadoed drawer. The bottom slides into dadoes cut in the sides and the front panel. The back fits into dadoes cut in the sides and rests on the bottom. Sides join front panel in rabbet joints. Dry-fit to check squareness, then glue-nail and set aside to dry.

(2) Front panel dadoed to take the side pieces; back butt-jointed between the two sides. The back will rest on the bottom panel, which in turn is supported by molding strips beneath it.

(3) Entirely butt-jointed drawer. This drawer can have a flush or overlapped panel attached to the front, either of which will hide the exposed end grain of the sides. This is the least strong drawer construction since parts depend upon glue, nails, or screws rather than fitted joints to hold them together.

(4) Undershelf drawers. These can be installed anytime. You can buy them ready-made, in kit form, or make drawer and support rails yourself. To hang a drawer under a shelf or cabinet, fasten a molding strip along the top edges of the drawer sides. Make an L-shaped runner of two cleats fastened together. For two drawers side-by-side, make a T-shaped runner of cleats. Give drawers extended front panels to hide cleat ends.

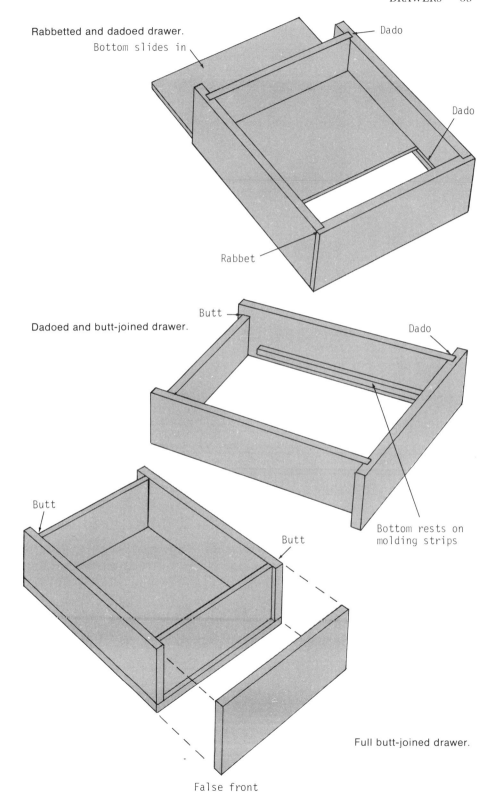

Rabbetted and dadoed drawer.
Bottom slides in

Dado

Dado

Rabbet

Butt

Dadoed and butt-joined drawer.

Dado

Butt

Butt

Bottom rests on
molding strips

Full butt-joined drawer.

False front

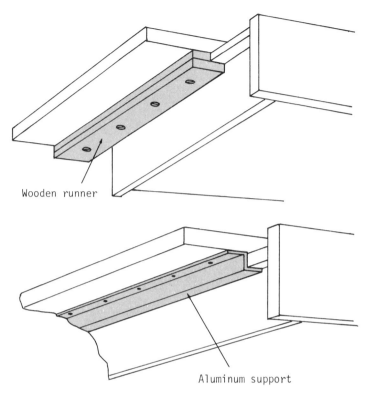

Wooden runner

Aluminum support

Under-shelf drawer supported by L-shaped runner made of cleats and molding strips. An alternate idea: support strip is of aluminium molding fastened to underside of shelf or wall cabinet.

You also can hang a drawer on support strips of aluminum available at hardware stores. Cut the metal strip to length with fine-tooth saw blade, and drill screw holes with a standard drill.

Drawer kits. Some people would rather buy precut and ready-to-assemble drawers than make them. And judging from the number of kits being marketed today, there are plenty of styles and sizes around for almost every storage purpose. You'll find them in department stores, hardware stores, building-supply centers, even variety stores.

All kits are designed to take the guesswork out of making and installing drawers, and most succeed. Size range is limited, though, so you are restricted in where you can use them. But if a project calls for more drawers than you'd care to make, investigate the kits available. You'll probably find one you can use.

8 | Wall Systems

BUILT-IN, FREE-STANDING, OR MODULAR—wall systems make the best use of vertical and horizontal storage spaces. The anatomy of a fully efficient arrangement is composed of

Shelves
Drawers
Cabinets
Open spaces
Closed spaces
Accessible work-surfaces, either
fold-out or stationary

Whether a wall system is distinctive enough to be the focal point of the room, or so unobtrusive it's barely noticeable, it will have one important feature—the styling of all the components will be consistent in line, trim, hardware.

Here are four examples that incorporate the fundamental principles of good, functional wall-system storage. Two are built-in, two are free-standing modulars with so much flexibility they can be arranged to fit any space in any room.

Stacked modulars of drawers, cabinets, and shelves present a united front. All doors are overlay, all drawer fronts are extended. Kickplates and recessed bases align. Slab frames are all the same thickness. Pulls and knobs are identical in style and color; sizes vary according to need.

The built-ins shown represent the best features all structures of this kind should have. First, styling is compatible with the surroundings. Second, spaces are shaped to best accommodate the items stored in them. And third, the systems make full use of the spaces available for them, either horizontally or vertically.

Another wall system, now a classic, arrived when tension devices made it possible to suspend shelves and cabinets from poles braced between floor and ceiling. Probably no other storage system was as enthusiastically welcomed as this one. Certainly nothing else exists that is more flexible, versatile, wholly useful for today's mobile citizenry. The heavy-duty metal poles, slotted to

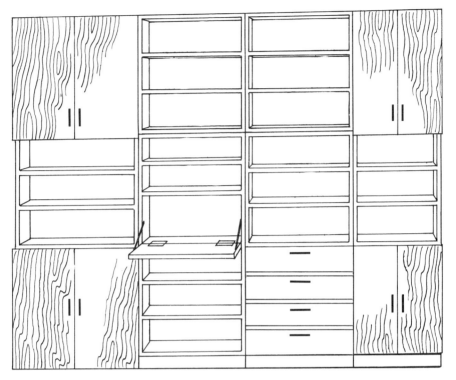

Modular wall systems can be organized to suit your particular needs.

take adjustable shelf brackets, are manufactured to hold incredibly heavy loads—rows of books, record collections, bar cabinets, desks with drop-down lids.

The shelf supports come in a variety of styles but more important, they're available for narrow, medium, or wide shelves and cabinets, all of which create total-use combinations of storage space for every place in the house from basement to master bedroom.

The tension device, a cap that fits over the ends of the poles, is composed of a strong steel spring, wide diameter surface discs (covered with a nonslip material), and an adjustable turn screw for tightening the discs against floor and ceiling. Some turn screws can be adjusted by hand; others require turning with a wrench. Though expensive, these poles assure a reliably strong suspension system and, if you'll be storing things that are very heavy, they're worth every cent.

You can also make your own tension poles of 2x3s outfitted at the top ends with spring-loaded tension caps made of wooden

Built-in wall system for a kitchen.

Built-in wall system for a traditional room.

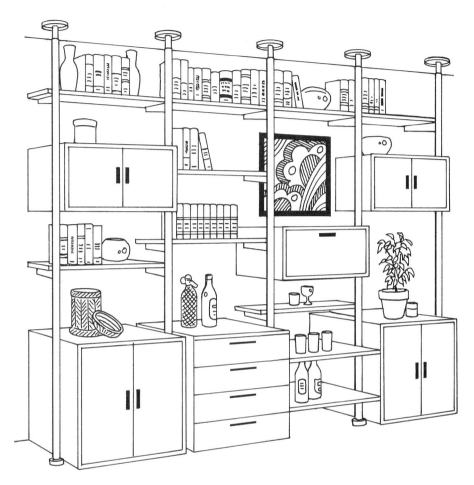

Slotted heavy-duty metal tension poles with adjustable supports hold an infinite variety of shelves and cabinets for books of all sizes, magazines, stereo equipment, record collections, plants, tools, and more. System is easy to dismantle, transport, set up somewhere else when you move.

dowels, metal tubing, and coiled steel spring. A wall system of this kind should be used for medium to light loads rather than extra heavy ones. Note, too, that since the tension caps are fashioned of several loose parts, use them on the top ends of the uprights. If placed on the bottom, they would keep falling out as you begin to wedge the poles into position. Pieces of inner tubing or rubberized shelf liner glued to the bottom ends of the posts will help keep them from slipping.

Shelves can be supported by dowels driven through holes in

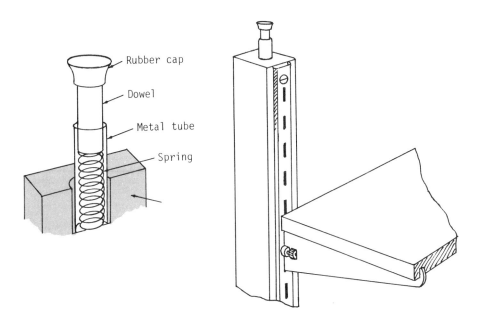

Spring-loaded 2x3s hold components of a shelf system in place between floor and ceiling. Make your own with wooden dowel, metal tube, and coiled steel spring.

the 2x3s. Notch corners of each shelf so the ends can fit through the 2x3s and rest on the dowels.

To install, form a back wall of rows of uprights spaced 30 inches apart. Using the same number of uprights, set a front-wall of uprights into position, keeping the front and back rows of posts apart by whatever is the width of the shelves. Drive dowels through holes in the uprights and set shelves on them. You will have a wall system that can be dismantled without leaving holes in existing walls, ceiling, or floor.

For a system that will carry even lighter loads, you can use 2x2s for the uprights, outfitting them with the same spring-loaded cap assembly.

Another ceiling-pressure device can be made by using threaded appliance levelers seated in holes drilled into the tops of 2x3s. Since these are not spring loaded, they will be tightened with a wrench. In this system, have a double row of uprights spaced 30 inches apart. Support shelves on pegged wood or metal shelf rests, or on metal clips suitable for slotted metal pilasters fastened to the 2x3s.

Wall systems can be totally or partially recessed. Sometimes this is an excellent way to counterbalance an awkward obstruction in the middle of a wall; or fill in an off-center alcove created by the protrusion of a closet situated in an adjoining room. The photograph shows how a wall system of shelves and cabinets is worked around a flue that pushed out into an otherwise well proportioned room. The entire wall is unified by having the base cabinets continue in one long unbroken line. The necessarily more shallow cabinets in the center hold small objects and books.

The wall system in the study (at right) shows how cabinets and shelves were fitted into an alcove formed by a closet in the adjacent room. Prefinished paneling curtains in the space over the wall system and covers the surrounding walls, giving the storage grouping a look of belonging and permanence. You can build a similar unit from scratch or use ready-made modulars such as these from Haag Cabinet Company, Inc.

A partially recessed wall system is used to disguise an awkward obstruction in the middle of a long wall. Wall paneling and shaped valances of plywood over the shelved alcoves continuous row of base cabinets. *Haag Cabinet Company.*

Fully recessed wall systems, whether modular or built-in, give a room balance if curtained-in at the top and sides with unifying wall covering of prefinished wall paneling or paper. *Haag Cabinet Company, Inc.; photo by Suter, Hedrich-Blessing.*

A wall system of ordinary bookcases can be arranged and partitioned so that, when overlay doors are added, the appearance and usefulness of the grouping is changed in a very interesting way. The doors in the system shown are of $1/2$ inch plywood covered in Con-Tact Brand peel-and-stick self adhesive vinyl. Doors are hung on lightweight loose pin no-mortise hinges and outfitted with surface mounted magnetic catches.

Concealing some but not all spaces in bookcases of this kind increases the amount of true storage you can wring from relatively small places. For instance, canned foods, soap, socks, and sweaters could be behind these doors and no one would know. In a small guest room, such an arrangement would provide plenty of storage places all in one location, cancelling the need for any other furnishings except bed and chair.

Modular cabinets and shelves can fill a long wall with open and closed spaces suitable for all kinds of storage. Note in the photo on page 72 the long doors of acrylic sheet on the cabinet at the left; they match the smokey tint of the record player cover. You can build your own modulars of $3/4$-inch plywood or use ready-mades such as these by Peak Designs Ltd., a British import.

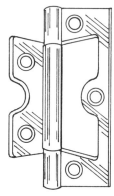

Bookcases fitted with doors create a simple wall system that provides spaces for storing things not ordinarily found in open bookcases; packaged foods, pots and pans, for example. Special hinge shown allows doors to be installed without mortising.

Modulars of shelves with doors form a wall system with long low base cabinet. Plastic doors (on the cabinet at left) and contrasting color on shelf sections make the whole unit more lively.

Two ladders with shelves hold books, TV, radio, and slab table top fitted with legs at the front. Use a tension device at top of ladder ends to hold uprights in position. *Photo courtesy Comark Plastics Division.*

In Chapter 5, we discussed ladders as being an excellent way to create light, airy wall systems capable of holding all kinds of shelves, hooks, hanging places for plants, lawn and garden tools, to name a few. In the photo above two ladders are used to hold shelves and an extended slab with legs (to make a table) in a game room. A full-wall system can be made of a series of such ladders to hold shelves and cabinets in children's rooms, dining rooms, dens. At the tops of the ladder uprights, install a tension device to hold the ladders between ceiling and floor.

An adaptation of the ladder arrangement concept is suggested by the assembly of modulars of rattan poles with trellis-like inserts which form the canopy and two corner units. A table between them completes the effect. Furniture design by Bob Thorpe for the Brown Jordan Treillage collection.

A wall system is also an ideal way to set up a workshop in basement or garage as shown on page 74. The modulars can be arranged in any combination of sizes and shapes. This group gives clues you can use to arrange cabinets and shelves made of plywood, stock lumber, and plastic laminate.

Wall systems in bathrooms produce ample storage in a room

Imported modulars, Tielsa System Alpha, are ready to assemble and install into workshop arrangement for home carpenters, artists, home gardeners. Drawer and door fronts are covered in plastic laminate. You can make such a wall system yourself.

that never seems to have enough space for supplies and appliances. A combination of open shelves, vanity base cabinet, and deep overhead cabinets shows how you can put every bit of available wall space to good use. Natural-finished knotty pine in this contemporary setting looks refreshing and assures easy upkeep when given several coats of low-sheen polyurethane varnish.

BUILDING A BUILT-IN. In creating a built-in wall system of shelves and cabinets, install a skeleton frame of 2x3s. Fasten

A bathroom wall system of open shelves and overhead cabinets creates a lighted grooming alcove, plus plenty of storage space right where it's needed. Notice that finger holes rather than pulls are used on doors and drawers, thus keeping all surfaces flat, more contemporary. *Designed by Allen Scruggs for Comark Plastics.*

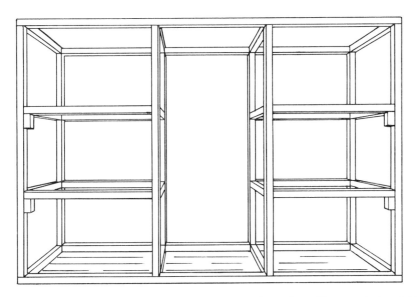

Skeleton frame for built-in wall system. Material is 2x3s throughout. Place central uprights (usually spaced 32 inches apart) where needed to support shelves, cabinets, or drawers. Nail 2×3 blocks to uprights to support toenailed ends of cross braces.

ceiling plates into position first, then drop plumb lines to determine where floor plates should go, then nail them to existing floor. Place uprights between ceiling and floors at all four corners, toe nail them into position. Next, nail cross braces between the end uprights at top, bottom, and wherever else you will need shelf supports. Central uprights should be placed spaced 32 inches apart on center if the mid portion of the built-in will be used to carry heavy loads.

Once the skeleton frame is completed, you can add shelves and create cabinet space by filling selected places inside the skeleton frame with sides and doors. Complete the built-in by installing a face frame over the 2x3s. Decorative moldings and hardware on cabinet doors, shelf edges, and face frame will create the finished style you want the unit to have.

Skeleton frames can take most configurations—tall and narrow or long and wide. The overall front-to-back depths of 18 to 24 inches are usually adequate for such systems, though of course, they can be made as deep or as shallow as space or personal preference dictate.

9 | Improving Existing Closets

THE USUAL COMPLAINT about a closet is that it's too small. What this really means, more often than not, is that the collection of things we want to stuff into it keeps getting bigger but the closet doesn't.

The compulsively spartan are the only ones who never have chaotic closets. That represents about one tenth of one per cent of the population who are happy with the closets they have—leaving the majority of homeowners desperate for more storage space and not sure where to find it. Is there a solution? Probably right there in the same old closet, full of wasted space that can be put to good use by making the opening larger and organizing the interior better.

Plan, first of all, to do away with the plain pipe rack look. The fond conviction that one long pole and one high shelf do a closet make is giving storage a bad name. What's needed here are many poles, many shelves, and many compartments. No corner, no inch of wall space shall be wasted, as you will see after we get on with making the opening larger.

Many closets have been and still are being made with narrow swing-out doors. These restrict accessibility to the contents inside. Nearly half the interior spaces of such closets are ignored because they are out of reach, out of sight. But if the opening is enlarged to the full width and height of the closet, dark corners and overhead spaces can be better utilized. The same closet will be capable of holding 40 to 50 per cent more than before.

The kind of door system capable of revealing nearly 100 per cent of a closet's (well organized) interior are full-height, 8-foot bi-fold doors. They are available in prefinished colors, styles, and sizes. Furthermore, they come in complete packages which include tracks, installed hardware, even decorative pulls.

Most are of precast steel so they cannot warp or otherwise change shape. They also come in 6-foot 8-inch heights as well as the 8-foot ones.

Manufacturers of bi-fold doors have made every effort to design and package them so that homeowners can handle the installation with as little effort and confusion as possible. Once you have the doors on-site, you can begin making a new opening in the old closet.

Material. You will need 2x4s for new header beams and support studs; plywood or stock lumber for shelves (or one of the prefinished, prepackaged shelf systems especially made for closets, but more about those later). Order firm, clear 1x4s for finish framing, and either flat or shaped moldings, 3 or 4 inches wide, for casing trim.

Procedure: Have the door system on hand before you begin. Mark on the wall the rough opening size required for the doors. For purposes of illustration and clarity, full-height, floor-to-ceiling bi-fold doors requiring a rough opening 61 inches wide will be used throughout. Systems for openings larger and smaller are also available. Styles are varied to suit almost every decor.

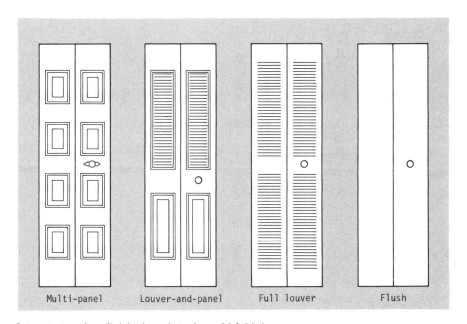

9-1. Styles of prefinished ready-to-hang bi-fold doors.

After marking the wall for opening size, remove the old door and pry off the door frame and jamb.

Following the rough opening lines previously marked, cut the wall material away until the old studs, header beam, and existing ceiling plate are exposed (Fig. 9-2). Use a wide chisel and hammer, or a saber saw. Make clean cuts in order to save patching later.

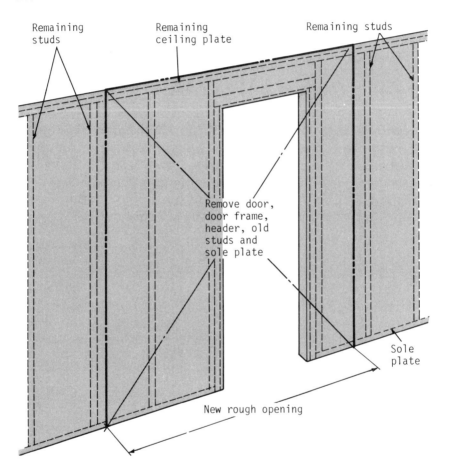

9-2. Enlarging a closet door opening and hanging bi-fold doors permits better utilizations of corners and dark spaces. First step is to rip out studs and door header, as shown.

Rip out unneeded studs and the old header and install a new header beam across the top of the opening. Use doubled 2x4s nailed together and fasten to the existing ceiling plate with 6-inch nails.

Now, support each end of the new header with 2x4s nailed to the existing studs (Fig. 9-3). Aim for these new supports to fit snugly between header and floor.

Next, nail finish framing of 1x4s to the underside of the new header and over the support studs (Fig. 9-3). Use firm, straight

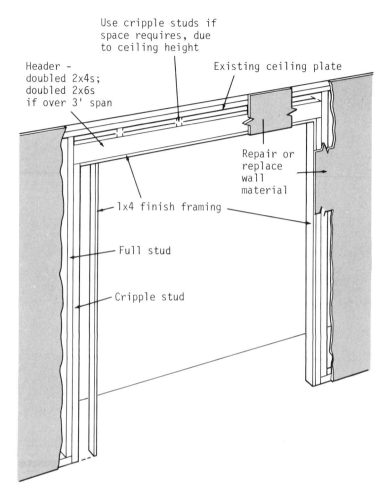

Use cripple studs if
space requires, due
to ceiling height

Header –
doubled 2x4s;
doubled 2x6s
if over 3' span

Existing ceiling plate

Repair or
replace
wall
material

1x4 finish framing

Full stud

Cripple stud

9-3. Framing the new opening for hanging bi-fold doors.

pieces of stock free of blemish and warp to assure that doors will fit properly. If shims have to be added to adjust size of the opening, add them behind these strips. Check with a spirit level to see that sides and overhead are level and square.

Installing doors. Fasten the metal overhead track to the underside of the header (Fig. 9-4). Check again for level positioning. If shims are needed at either end, place washers over the track screws. (Washers go between track and overhead frame.)

At this point, fill in cut wall material and cover the new header with wallboard or plaster. Prepare the exterior for final finishing.

Install the doors in the overhead track to test for level and hanging balance (Fig. 9-4). Doors come with adjustable hanger devices

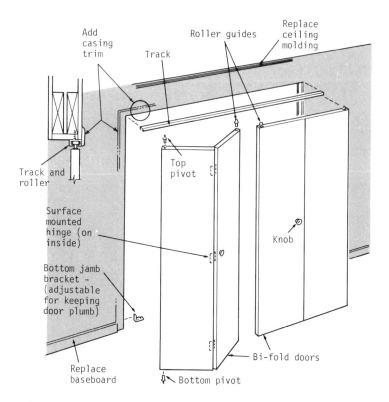

Add casing trim

Track

Roller guides

Replace ceiling molding

Track and roller

Top pivot

Surface mounted hinge (on inside)

Knob

Bottom jamb bracket - (adjustable for keeping door plumb)

Replace baseboard

Bottom pivot

Bi-fold doors

9-4. Installing bi-fold doors. Casing, or face trim, is added after the doors are adjusted.

for correcting minor inaccuracies in fitting at top and bottom.

Casing, or face trim, should be added around the opening after the doors are adjusted and operating properly (Fig. 9-4). Trim can cover most of the ragged edges made by cutting the wall material away. Use shaped or flat molding, and miter corners. Final-finish patched wall areas and casing.

ORGANIZING CLOSETS. Many talented men and women make a good living designing closet interiors for other people. To ensure the finished closet will be all that you envisioned, consider how you will use the space. Clothing, shoes, accessories, luggage all require different amounts of space. Therefore, plan ahead as to where shelves, clothes rods, brackets, cabinets will eventually be installed. See Fig. 9-5 for various ways to organize your now-new closet.

There are also prefinished, precut, adjustable shelving systems which, like prefabricated doors, are in bountiful supply. They come in a wide range of shapes, widths, lengths, and colors. Predominant materials are steel with baked-on enamel finish, particleboard with bonded vinyl finishes, and steel rod mesh coated in tough vinyl.

Makers of these ready-to-assemble systems include appropriate hardware and fasteners. Home centers, hardware, and building-supply stores stock them in serve-yourself racks.

Closet lighting. A wall switch just outside the closet is the most convenient and often less costly way to illuminate the interior.

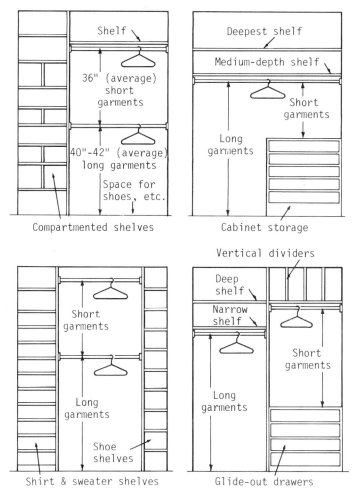

9-5. Compartmentalize a closet for best use of space.

A recessed overhead light will be the most useful. A switch with its own pilot light would be a definite asset; it reminds you when the light has been left on.

Of course, any number of lights can be installed in large- and medium-size closets. (Very shallow ones are illuminated by room lighting.) Lights can be installed on walls, ceiling, even under shelves provided you shield the bulbs and take care not to have them too close to materials that can burn or scorch.

Connect all closet lighting to normal household current. Since this requires the knowledge of a professional, do not attempt it yourself unless you know exactly what you're doing.

For general-purpose lighting in clothes closets, remote on-off systems are ideal. The light comes on as the door opens and switches off when the door closes. Of these, the wired-in systems are the greatest pleasure to own. They are also the most expensive because an electrician must install them. An instant on-off switch is recessed into the door frame and is activated by the motion position of the door. Lights wired to the remote switch can be placed in ceiling or walls. Electrical supply shops carry these door switch systems.

Automatic closet lights are self-contained units that can be surface-mounted to the door stile or the frame. These systems consist of a socket, extension cord, and on-off pressures switch which rests against some portion of the door. These lighting systems require that an outlet be located inside the closet.

Another lighting possibility is the wireless, battery-operated fixture with pull-chain. These use two standard "D" batteries. The fixtures can be mounted anywhere on closet walls or ceiling.

10 | Building New Closets

CLOSETS ARE PERSONAL places which all of us want with a fervor. Nobody escapes the hunger for more. The compulsively organized spend hours arranging, stacking, labeling. They sleep better just knowing everything is in its proper place. Equally driven are the packrats who can't throw anything away, yet never stop collecting.

It's not surprising, then, that the closets already built into our homes never measure up to need. One of the most effective and personally satisfying ways to have enough closets is to build them yourself. Thankfully, materials and fittings are close at hand in the many building-supply stores and home centers across the country. Moreover, prefabricated door and shelf systems make it easy for home carpenters to tackle jobs that once only professionals handled.

Closets can be built almost anywhere. You needn't be limited by the size of your home whether it's one room or twenty.

Closets can be big, small, shallow, or deep. They can hold brooms and mops or serve as hideaway home offices.

Closets can line the walls of a room and become in the process effective insulators and sound buffers. They can be built into a corner, or jut out from a wall to function as both closet and room divider.

In this chapter are three classic closets to build: the wall-to-wall, the in-corner, the room divider (Fig. 10-1).

You know from experience that walls are seldom plumb and floors and ceilings rarely level. So in building any closet, rely on plumb line and spirit level as diligently as an explorer does his compass. Check each stud and plate before and after nailing it into place.

Emphasis will be on full-width floor-to-ceiling folding doors that are prefabricated, prefinished. These assemblies come complete with component parts, hardware, and adjustable fittings. Doors are designed in styles that are suitable for every setting, and have finishes that you can leave as is or repaint. If full-height

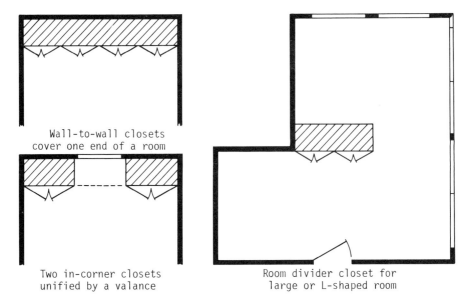

Wall-to-wall closets
cover one end of a room

Two in-corner closets
unified by a valance

Room divider closet for
large or L-shaped room

10-1. Classic closet configurations.

doors do not suit your needs, 80-inch doors are available in all styles and finishes.

Closet framework needs sturdy moorings. Though made to look built-in, new closets are in essence add-ons that lack the deep root-system of a building's initial structure. They need to be firmly anchored to existing studs, joists, and beams; nailing just into plaster or wallboard is not good enough. If, because of the closet's dimensions or placement in a room, some part of the frame rests where there is no stud or beam to nail into, then toggle bolts or expansion anchors will have to be used.

Floors, on the other hand, are usually surfaced with wood that is thick enough and firm enough to nail into directly. If the floors are of concrete, either bare or surfaced with thin wood parquetry, attach floor plates with masonry nails. Very old wood floors are often too weak or spongy to hold fasteners firmly for long. It's wise in such instances to nail into a floor joist.

Existing baseboards should be removed, otherwise you will have the dickens of a time framing-out around them. Carefully pry off moldings and board back to their respective seams, or nearest corner. Keep intact until you are ready to cut and refit them around the base of the closet.

Materials. Closet framing of 2x3s on 24-inch centers is becoming popular. Where a closet framework has the additional support of existing walls, ceiling, and floor, there's no reason why this lighter construction shouldn't be considered over the more traditional 2x4s on 16-inch centers. However, in buildings that are subjected to much vibration, from outside traffic or lively neighbors overhead, traditional framing methods may be the soundest way to ensure against unexpected shifting and a parade of alignment problems. The choice of framing method is up to you, although there are two situations that demand the 2x4 traditional approach: if the closet doors are to be mirrored; if the doors are to span an opening wider than 6 feet. Such doors are heavy and need sturdy framing, especially across the front. The remainder of the framework can be of 2x3s on 24-inch centers if you want to combine both methods in order to save time and material.

In this chapter, the traditional approach, 2x4s on 16-inch centers, will be used so that accompanying text and illustration are not a confusing jumble of either-or dimensions.

To enclose closet framework use gypsum board, often called wallboard or prefinished paneling. Both materials come in 4x8 ft. sheets. Wallboard can be painted, papered, or covered in anything from carpeting to damask. Prefinished paneling comes in a range of colors, textures, and patterns that is almost limitless. This smooth-surfaced material is also ideal for closet interiors. Dust won't cling to it, clothes can't snag on it, and the color never grows dull and dark.

To make a closet look as though it were an architectural part of the room from the beginning, follow these simple rules: Use trim around the top of the closet that matches trim around the rest of the room. If no ceiling-wall trim exists, cover the wall-ceiling juncture with quarter-round molding painted to match the ceiling. Finish the base of the closet with baseboard and molding identical with that used throughout the room. Also, select doors that blend with the style of the room (Fig. 10-2).

WALL-TO-WALL CLOSET. This is the simplest closet to build because existing walls, floor, and ceiling provide you with ready-built supports on five sides. To complete, add front framework and full-height doors, or 80-inch doors if you prefer.

The size of the opening is determined by the rough-opening dimensions required by the door plus allowance for the 1x4

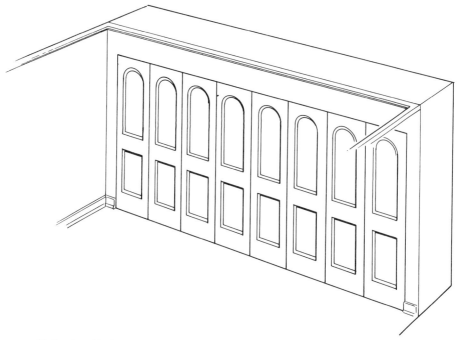

10-2.   A wall of closets is an attractive and practical addition to a room.

finish-framing inside it. Make the closet as deep as you want. An interior depth of 22 to 24 inches is ample for hanging garments.

Material. In addition to the prefab doors and related hardware, you will use 2x4s for all framework and cross braces, strips of 1x4 for finish framing, flat or shaped 3- to 4-inch molding for casing trim, and wallboard or paneling for enclosing the framework.

Procedure. Cut out baseboard to accommodate framework. Install 2x4 ceiling plate (Fig. 10-3). Fasten to existing joists with nails, but if there's no joist to nail into, use toggles.

If you have no helper, make a "dead man" support of a length of 2x4 and pieces of plywood (Fig. 10-4) to brace the ceiling plate as you work.

Support the installed ceiling plate with verticals of 2x4 nailed into the existing wall studs. Again, if no studs are available use toggles or other fasteners appropriate for the type of wall material.

To give the ceiling plate extra support, nail short 2x4 blocks to top end of vertical supports.

Fasten the 2x4 floor plate across the span directly under the ceiling plate. Drop a plumb line from the ceiling plate to deter-

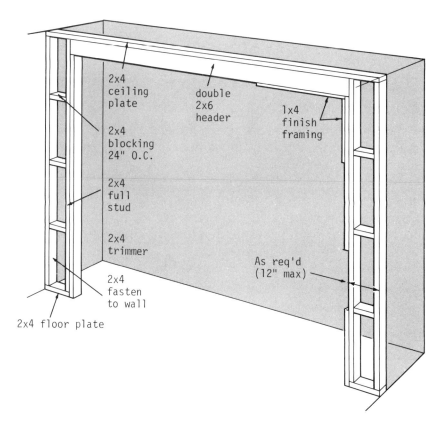

2x4
ceiling
plate

double
2x6
header

1x4
finish
framing

2x4
blocking
24" O.C.

2x4
full
stud

2x4
trimmer

As req'd
(12" max)

2x4
fasten
to wall

2x4 floor plate

10-3. Basic frame for full-height doors in wall-to-wall closet.

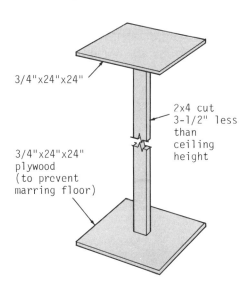

3/4"x24"x24"

2x4 cut
3-1/2" less
than
ceiling
height

3/4"x24"x24"
plywood
(to prevent
marring floor)

10-4. Dead-man support aids in holding ceiling plate in place when working alone.

mine the exact position of the floor plate. (You will cut out main portion of the floor plate later.)

Cut two sections of 2x4 to act as frame supports. Fit them snugly between floor and ceiling plates. Position them out from vertical supports as required for proper rough opening dimensions. Toenail to ceiling and floor plates.

Cut short lengths of 2x4 for cross braces between verticals. Toenail to wall stud; end-nail to frame support from outside the support.

At this point, if you will be using 80-inch doors instead of full-height doors, install a soffit frame; see Fig. 10-5. Then continue the procedure that follows.

Install header of double 2x4s nailed together back-to-back. Prop with dead man support as you work.

Cut two lengths of 2x4 to act as vertical header supports. Snug-fit verticals between header and floor plate. Nail them to vertical frame supports.

Cut excess floor plate away between the verticals that form the openings.

Install 1x4 finish framing strips to underside of header and down sides of header supports.

Check with plumb line and spirit level to assure opening is level and square. Place shims between finish frame and header supports; between finish framing and header, if needed.

To install doors, follow these procedures and see Fig. 9-4:

Install metal track for doors to underside of header finish framing. Check again for level and positioning. If shims are needed place washers over track screws. (Washers between track and finish framing.)

Now, cover exposed framework with wallboard or paneling. Prepare for final finishing; fill, tape and cover seams if wall-board, add molding strips if paneling.

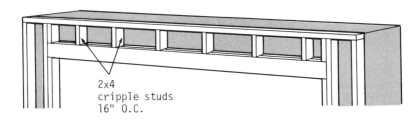

2x4
cripple studs
16" O.C.

10-5. Basic frame for 80-inch doors in wall-to-wall closet.

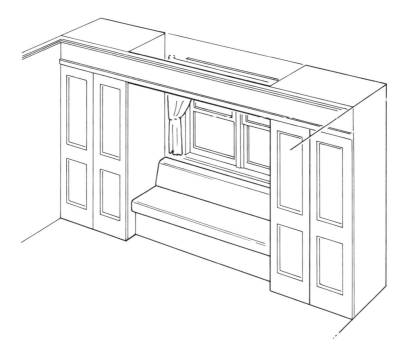

10-6. Two in-corner closets with space between for sofa, bed, or desk.

Install doors in overhead track; test for level, hanging balance, smooth operation. Doors come with adjustable hanger devices for correcting minor inaccuracies in fitting at top and bottom.

Casing, or face trim, should be added after doors are hung and wallboard or paneling is final-finished. Miter trim at corners. Final-finish casing trim.

IN-CORNER CLOSET. When you cannot enclose an entire wall with closets, use this one. The framing principle is much the same for wall-to-wall closets except that the free end will be given extra support by cross braces and double 2x4s at the front corner (see Fig. 10-6).

Material. Have doors on hand before you begin framing. All the same material will be used in this construction as in the wall-to-wall closet. And you will need wallboard or paneling to cover free end and other exposed framework.

Procedure. Cut out the baseboard to accommodate the framework. Determine rough opening size according to the doors you will use. Plan outside dimension of the closet to be 24 inches

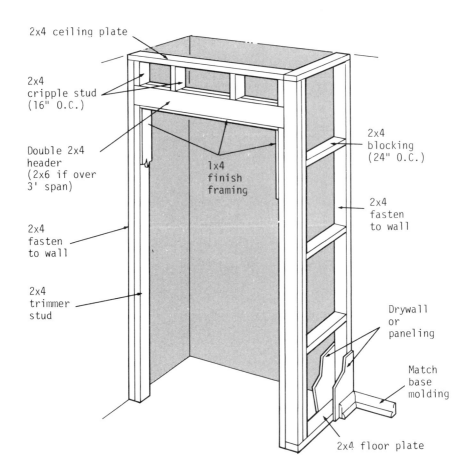

2x4 ceiling plate

2x4
cripple stud
(16" O.C.)

Double 2x4
header
(2x6 if over
3' span)

1x4
finish
framing

2x4
blocking
(24" O.C.)

2x4
fasten
to wall

2x4
fasten
to wall

2x4
trimmer
stud

Drywall
or
paneling

Match
base
molding

2x4 floor plate

10-7. Basic frame for in-corner closet using 80-inch doors.

(front to back) so half a sheet of wallboard or paneling will cover the end of the closet.

Install the 2x4 ceiling plate, with nails if there are joists, with toggles if not.

Support the ceiling plate with vertical 2x4s nailed to the existing wall stud. If no stud, use an anchor appropriate for type of wall material. Use a plumb line to determine accurate positioning of this vertical.

Install the corner ceiling plate at right angle to the previously installed ceiling plate. Check for square and nail or bolt to existing ceiling.

Support wall end of corner ceiling plate with vertical 2x4 nailed, or anchored, to existing wall and floor.

Drop plumb line from end of corner plate to determine the position of the floor plate. Cut short length of 2x4 for the floor plate and nail to the existing floor; toenail to the vertical support.

To install outer corner support of double 2x4s, drop a plumb line from the ceiling plate to determine proper positioning. Toenail to ceiling plates and floor plate.

Cut short lengths of 2x4 to act as braces. Fasten between wall vertical and corner support.

At this point, if you are installing 80-inch doors instead of full-height doors, install a soffit frame. Refer back to Fig. 10-5. Then continue with procedures that follow:

Install a header of double 2x4s nailed to the ceiling plate.

Cut two lengths of 2x4 to act as vertical header supports. Snug-fit them between header and floor. Nail to the vertical frame supports.

Nail 1x4 finish framing strips to the underside of header and down sides of header supports.

Check with plumb line and spirit level to assure opening is level and square. Place shims between finish framing and header supports; between finish framing and header, if needed.

To install doors, refer back to Fig. 9-4 and procedures used for installing doors in wall-to-wall closet.

Enclose closet end and framing with wallboard or paneling. Since the outside dimension of the closet is 24 inches (front to back wall) you will use half a sheet of 4x8-foot material. Mark and cut on the waste side of the cutting line.

Two in-corner closets are ideal for small rooms; the space between them can be used for a bed, sofa, or desk. Often such an arrangement is the only way to have adequate storage as well as space for a necessary piece of furniture.

A valance between the two closets gives a built-in look to the whole wall. The room will look less chopped-up if you use this

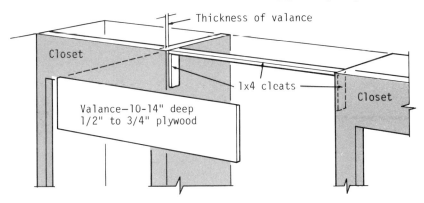

10-8. Use $^1/_2$- or $^3/_4$-inch plywood, or wallboard, for valance. Install support cleats of 1x4 strips to the end wall of closets; make cleats 1 inch shorter than depth of valance. Nail horizontal 1x4 strip to cleats.

unifying technique. Make the valance fairly deep, from 10 to 14 inches. Cover and trim it to match closet. (See Fig. 10-8.)

ROOM DIVIDER CLOSET. From a materials and construction standpoint, this closet is more involved than the preceding two. Those could be created by framing-out one side (across front) or at the most, two sides (front and one end). Here, you will need to frameout three sides—front, back, and one end.

Although the room divider closet is less simple than the others, it has more advantages. In the first place, space limitations and room layout may be such that this is the best configuration to use. Furthermore, you gain not only more storage but get extra wall space (and privacy) on the other side.

With space and material costs being what they are today, many houses and apartments are being built with fewer interior partitions. The L-shaped room is a prime example of the open floor plan builders and designers are using to create the illusion of greater space when actually there may be less than usual. In such

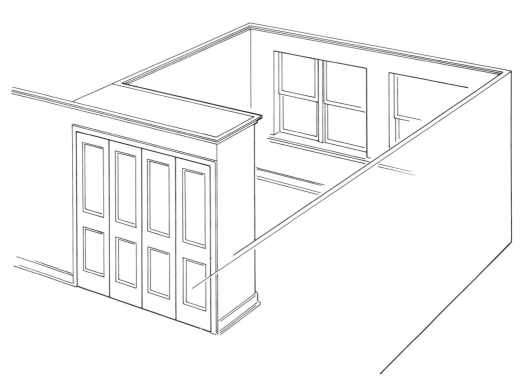

10-9. Room-divider closet creates two rooms and storage space at the same time.

situations, a room divider that's also a closet has more practical advantages than a thin partition or folding screen arranged for the same purpose.

The key to building this kind of closet successfully is to keep all framing members plumb and square, and to check at each step along the way to see that they are. Use a plumb line rather than trusting your eye.

Materials. In addition to the prefab door system, you will use 2x4s for all portions of the framework—or use 2x3s on 24-inch centers along the back wall of the closet. Also, you'll need 1x4s for finish framing, molding strips for casing trim, and wallboard or paneling for enclosing the framework.

Procedure. Cut out the baseboard to accommodate the framework. Determine rough opening size according to the doors you will use. Plan the outside of the closet dimension to be 24 inches

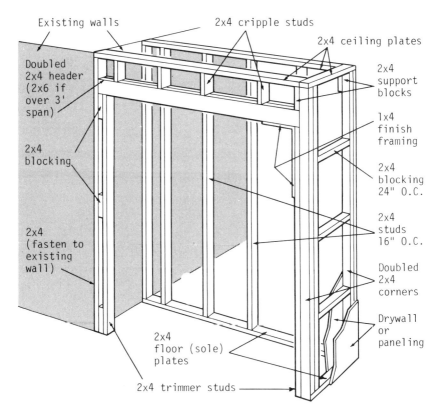

10-10.   Completed framing for room divider closet. Depth can be adjusted according to amount of space available.

front to back so half a sheet of wallboard or paneling will cover the free end of the closet.

Install ceiling plates: one across front, one across back, one across free end (Fig. 10-10). Check for level and square. Nail ceiling plates to joists, or if none, use toggles.

Nail, or anchor, vertical 2x4s to the existing wall to act as ceiling plate supports.

To give ceiling plates extra support at back, nail short 2x4 block to upper end of vertical.

Drop a plumb line from ceiling plates to determine position of floor plates across back, front, and end. (Main portion of front floor plate will be cut out later.)

Install verticals of double 2x4s between floor and ceiling plates at each corner of free end. Check for plumb. Toenail in place. (See Fig. 10-10.)

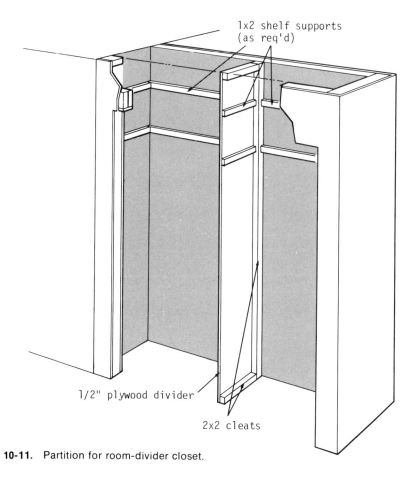

10-11. Partition for room-divider closet.

End-nail cross braces of short 2x4s between corner verticals. Frame-in the back wall with 2x4s on 16-inch centers; toenail to floor and ceiling plates.

Cleats of 1x4s between verticals on existing wall are optional. Place them where you will need supports for clothes rods, shelves, and the like.

If you plan to use 80-inch doors instead of full-height ones install soffit framework now, before installing header. Refer back to Fig. 10-5.

Cut excess portion of floor plate away.

Install header of double 2x4s nailed to the ceiling plate.

Snug-fit vertical 2x4s between header and floor. Nail to corner support and to the vertical 2x4 fastened to existing wall. Toenail to header and floor.

Nail 1x4 finish framing strips to underside of header and down sides of header supports.

Check with plumb line and spirit level to assure opening framework is level and square. Place shims between finish framing and header supports; between finish framing and header if needed.

Enclose closet framework with wallboard or paneling. Prepare for final-finishing: fill, tape, and cover seams, add metal corner-bead at outside corners of wallboard. Add molding strips if paneling is used.

To install doors, refer back to Fig. 9-4 and follow procedures used for doors on wall-to-wall closet.

If you're going to have partitions in the closet, install them before enclosing the framework (see Fig. 10-11). Then compartmentalize the closet for best use of the space.

11 | Two-Leaf Swing-Out Shelves

LONG NARROW STORAGE SHELVES are often the most convenient. Everything—from office supplies to canned soups to toys—is easier to put away and to retrieve if arranged in single rows rather than jumbled one behind another in a deep recess. But since few homes have that kind of stretch-out room available, one of the best answers is a system of shallow shelf units that open and close upon each other like pages in a book.

The unit shown here is 6 feet high, 20 inches wide, and, when closed, 22 inches deep. It is designed to hold such things as canned and packaged goods and gardening supplies. However, you can adapt the same design principle for small wall-hung systems by scaling down the dimensions to whatever proportions you want. Such mini-versions could hold a multitude of kitchen gadgets, hobby supplies, or shaving and grooming gear.

To assure smooth operation of the swing-outs in the full-size unit, continuous hinges join the separate sections. Shutter or butt hinges would do for smaller wall-hung units.

Also note in the full-size unit that the two swing-out sections are 2 inches shorter than the stationary rear section. This is done to accommodate a swivel caster with tread under the center swing-out and to give the door, which rests against it, ample above-floor clearance.

Prefinished wall paneling can be used to cover the storage door outside as a means to get instant style and color options with no effort on your part. The panel is framed by a border of bead molding mitered at the corners to give the project a crisp, professional look.

The door can have a D-shaped handle, a decorative pull or, if you want no hardware showing, a hand-hold cut in the end vertical.

Shelves in the center and rear section are $9^1/_4$ inches deep, while those in the door are a mere $3^1/_2$ inches; adequate for most cans and small packages. Our full-size unit shows three shelves (plus bottoms) in each section, but actual number and placement should be dictated by household need.

Shelves in the stationary rear section don't need lips or guardrails, but those in the movable sections do. Use dowels, elastic rope, lath strips, molding, or strips of clear plastic.

Shelves can be supported in a number of ways: By dadoes cut in the verticals, by wood cleats, slotted metal pilasters, or flanged metal pegs (shelf rests) set into predrilled holes. Dadoes in the center and rear sections would be ideal because such joining gives the whole assembly extra strength and stability. Use flanged peg supports in the door section so the shelves can be spaced close together or far apart whenever you need to adjust them.

Material. Use 1x4 stock for the storage door, and 1x10 stock for the center and rear sections. Stress to your dealer that you want clear lumber, since each section's edges must fit flat and true against the other. Material for the shelves can be the same as the framing stock, or can be $3/4$-inch plywood. Backings can be $1/4$-inch material.

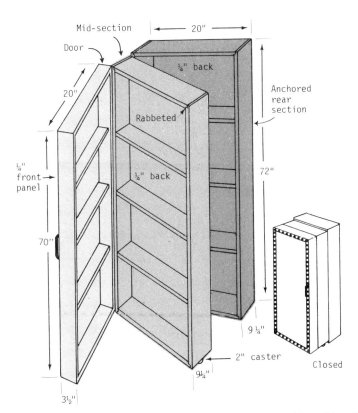

11-1. The two-leaf swing-out is simply a system of narrow shelves hinged together like pages in a book to form compact but highly accessible storage spaces.

Rear section assembly. This is a stationary unit that will rest against or be anchored to an existing wall. It is $9^1/_4$ inches deep, not counting backing, which can be $^1/_4$-inch plywood or hardboard. The frame is of 1"x10" stock with rabbeted top, dadoes for shelves, and a 1x2 kickplate. To allow for existing baseboard, notch the lower back ends of the verticals and adjust the dimensions of the bottom shelf. (See "Getting Around Baseboards," Chapter 5.) Glue-nail framing together and slide shelves into place, but do not permanently fasten them or the kickplate until well into the final assembly step. (You may have to remove the shelves to adjust alignment of the fully assembled unit after the swing-out sections are attached.) Glue-nail backing into place and set section aside to dry.

Center section assembly. Essentially this is a swing-out shelf arrangement that is $9^1/_4$" deep. The frame is of 1x10 stock with rabbeted top and butt-jointed bottom set flush between ends of verticals. The verticals are dadoed for shelves. Remember that this section is 2 inches shorter than the rear section in order to accommodate a caster on its underside. Although there is a $^1/_4$ inch backing, stored items will need to have guardrails or lips on the open side of the shelves. Cut a D-shaped hand hold in the free end of the vertical at a height above floor level that's most comfortable for you. Fit and glue-nail all parts together, add backing, and set aside to dry. With the unit lying flat, install the caster by centering it 4 inches in from the edge of the free end. Fasten the continuous hinge along the vertical edge that will be joined to the rear section.

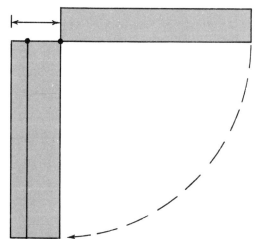

11-2. Allow for clearance at hinged side of swing-out.

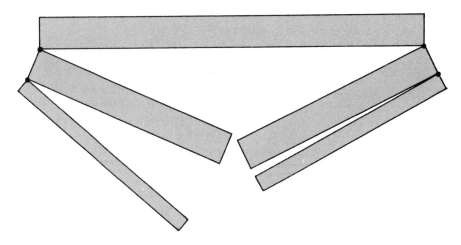

11-3. Double swing-out version, like the single swing-out, can be as large or as small as space permits.

Door section assembly. This is a shallow box that is $3^1/_2$ inches deep. The frame is of 1x4 stock with rabbeted top, butt-jointed bottom set flush between ends of verticals. It will be fitted with narrow shelves set on pegged supports. This section also is 2 inches shorter than the rear section. If you prefer not to have a door handle, cut a D-shaped handhold in the free end of the vertical, and *then* drill shelf support peg holes. Glue-nail the frame together, add backing, and set aside to dry. Install a continuous hinge along the vertical edge that will be joined to the center section. Turn the unit flat and glue-nail the prefinished panel into place over backing. (Make panel $^1/_4''$ smaller all around than outer dimensions of the frame to allow for bead molding border.) Miter molding at corners, fasten to backing with glue and brads. Weight or clamp and set aside to dry.

Final assembly. Bring all three sections together on site for a trial run. With hinges held in place by only a few screws in each hinge leaf, attach the center section to the rear section, and attach the door section to the center section. Check for square, plumb alignment, and smooth swing-out operation. Next, place a few heavy cans and packages inside each section and check behavior of the unit again in its weighted condition. Note if the hinges, caster, or base of the rear section need to be shimmed. Floors are not always level as you well know, so make sure the caster is in proper contact with the floor at all times. If after preliminary testing you decide to anchor the rear section to the wall, the unit's overall balance, and especially the caster's floor contact, may be affected. Therefore, remove all weights, take shelves out of the rear section, and install an anchor appropriate for type of wall. Be prepared to readjust shims for unit balance, and caster-to-floor contact. When all parts operate smoothly together, install shelves and kickplate in the rear section. Then final-drive all hinge screws. You can sand, seal, and finish the unit after it's assembled, but it would be much easier to do most or all of it before the three sections are joined together.

12 | Extra Storage for Kitchens

HAVING THE RIGHT kind of storage spaces in kitchens is an eternal challenge. Big kitchens with roomy cabinets and closets appear to be well organized, but how efficient are they? Are the many utensils essential for meal preparation easy to reach? Usually not, for storage units in such places are not only deep, but are situated above and below the most convenient work-surface level.

Small kitchens, on the other hand, present another kind of problem. Although equipment and tools are never far away, they soon become a mass of disorganized clutter unless constantly policed.

MAKE A BATCH OF BOXES. One of the most recent, and popular, concepts in kitchen storage is complete openness—letting it all show. Another is compartmentalization—letting the object determine the proportion of the space it's to occupy, thereby eliminating precarious stacking of dissimilar shapes. The result of such an arrangement is a wall montage of random containers jutting here and receding there; stretching horizontally and vertically to accommodate a variety of things like bulky soup tureens; tiny spice jars, flat trays.

Once you begin to formulate how a series of different sized boxes can best be grouped, you will see that empty spaces will form between them. These are just as useful for storage as the boxes themselves. For instance, the arrangement here consists of twelve boxes, but there are fourteen storage cavities. One is occupied by the slotted stemware rack. Another holds the clock.

Such a free-form system as this is highly personalized, of course, and any set of specifics can only be offered as a guideline to shapes, sizes, uses.

As for construction and design techniques, they are simplicity itself. You make a batch of boxes, fasten them to the wall and to each other, and fill them with whatever you want. Patience is the

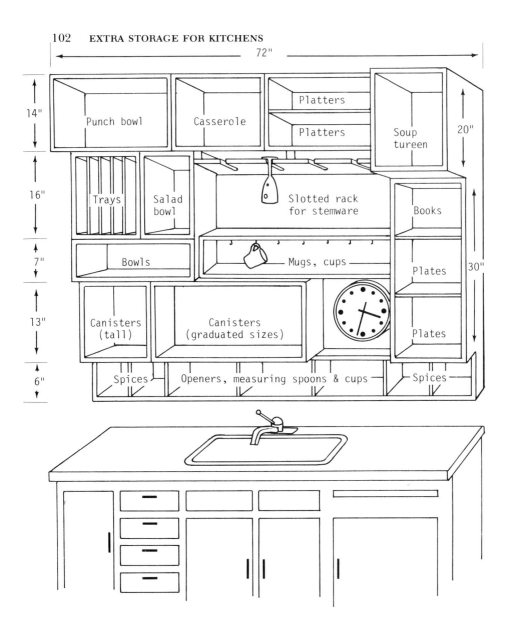

12-1. A collection of separate boxes, some deep, some shallow, some tall, some wide, creates a free-form assemblage of spaces, each with a storage purpose.

key. If you have that and enjoy building boxes, this project is for you.

For illustrative purposes, this wall arrangement is situated over a sink countertop that's 5 feet wide. It fills the space between the top of the backsplash and the ceiling. Sizes graduate from shallow recesses at the bottom to deeper ones higher up—where large and less frequently used items are stored. Mark the wall to indicate where the outside boundaries of the assemblage will be. Then make a layout on paper of how you plan to arrange the boxes, assigning each one a number.

Material. There's almost no limit to what you can use. Scrap lumber or plywood you have on hand will get you started. Plywood will be the best choice for the deep boxes at the top while 1x4s and 1x2s will serve for the rest. Each box should have its own backing of $1/4$-inch plywood.

Procedure. Join a box's edges together by any method that best suits you. Rabbet, miter, or butt-joints. Butts are suitable because the boxes will support each other to a large extent. Cut dadoes for shelves and partitions, or use manufactured metal channel strips, or pegs. As each box is assembled, number it according to your layout plan. As you begin fastening the boxes into position on the wall, start with the top row, working across the span rather than vertically. This way, when you reach the bottom row, if the boxes have to be shimmed or planed down for proper fit, the lower ones are easier to get at. If you feel the boxes should also be joined together here or there, use wood screws.

Finishing. Sand, seal and finish the boxes before you put them up. After they're in place, you can easily touch up any gouges or scratches that occurred during installation. The boxes can be painted or given a natural finish, depending upon preference. Their edges can be trimmed with molding, colored tape, or contrasting-color paint. Some backs, such as those that will be behind clear glassware, can be covered with colorful paper.

SLOTTED STEMWARE RACK. Wine, sherbet, and sherry glasses have their own place inside the wall of boxes. This rack is 23 inches long, 12 inches wide, and contains six slots. Infinite size variations are possible for many types of stemmed glassware. Racks for this purpose should be situated in a separate overhead location where the glass cannot be struck by other objects.

Material. The slotted panel is made of $3/4$-inch plywood. The top frame mounting strips are of 1x2s.

Procedure. With saber or coping saw, cut slots in the plywood panel, ending the openings about 2 inches from the back edge. Make slots $3/4$ inch wide and space them 2 inches apart. Allow space at each side and up the middle of the panel to accommodate mounting strips which are glue-nailed into place.

Attach the rack to the bottoms of boxes forming the top part of cavity in which the rack will be located. Use wood screws or nails.

Finishing. Sand, seal, and coat the entire rack with final finish, either paint or stain. The surface should be smooth but not slippery. Buff with steel wool if it appears to need a bit of roughing.

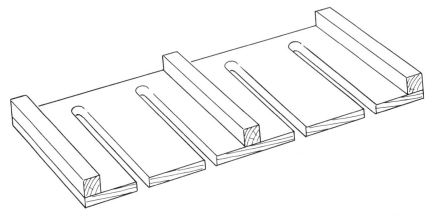

12-2.   Slotted stemware rack holds glasses securely in a space within the wall of boxes.

13 | More Storage in Bathrooms

EACH YEAR the number of new products for use and storage in bathrooms keeps increasing, but the size of the room itself remains the same. The two projects in this chapter—vanity base cabinet and hair-grooming center—are designed to help you gain storage flexibility in an area of the house that's traditionally more restricted than any other.

VANITY BASE CABINET. It's designed to be fitted with one of the readymade china/marble integral tops available from mail order houses and home centers. This one is 31 by 19 inches, suitable for a base 30 inches wide and 18 inches deep.

It consists of a basic box frame on a recessed base and is enclosed in plywood that can be painted or given a natural finish. The back is left open to allow for drain lines.

Material. The box frame is made of 2x2 stock. Side panels, doors, facing strip, and floor are of $^3/_4$ inch hardwood plywood. The recessed base frame is composed of 2x4s set on edge.

Procedure. With 2x2s, construct the box frame by first making two rectangles, lap-jointed at ends and glue-nailed together. Place 2x2 uprights between top and bottom rectangles and butt-join them together.

Make recessed base of 2x4s laid on edge and butt-jointed. Use glue and wood screws.

Cut **floor and glue-nail to base, keeping it flush at sides and back** but with a $2^1/_2$-inch overhang at front.

Set the box frame onto the base, keeping all edges flush. Glue-nail into place. With wood putty, fill all gaps that appear between frame and base.

Fasten overlap facing strip across the front of box frame with wood screws driven from inside the frame.

Cut two side panels with notches at the bottom front edge to allow for $2^1/_2$-by-$3^1/_2$-inch toe space.

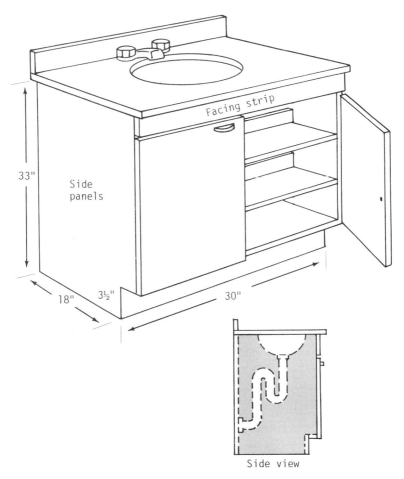

13-1. Neat, trim vanity base cabinet is designed to be fitted with ready-made china/marble top you can order by mail or find at home centers. Tops come in a variety of colors.

Nailing from outside, attach side panels to the frame and sides of the recessed base. Set nails and fill depressions with wood filler. Let dry, then sand smooth.

Sand and seal all interior surfaces now, while it's easy to get at them. Also, cover all exposed plywood edges with extra care, using the spackle-and-sanding method. Make sure they are thoroughly covered and smooth.

Cut and prepare two overlap doors for fitting and hanging. Using concealed hinges, mark hinge positions on cabinet interior and doors and mortise surfaces to receive hinge leaf. Spackle and sand raw edges of doors completely so they will be water-resistant.

Install interior supports for drawers, shelves, or partitions, but do not outfit the inside until plumbing connections are made.

When the cabinet is ready to be installed, disconnect existing sink and set the base into position. Check for firm, level fit against floor and wall. Shim where necessary.

Install integral top, faucet set, and make plumbing connections. Add interior shelves or whatever, fit and final-hang doors. Install magnetic catches and door pulls.

Finish. Give all edges and surfaces a thorough final sanding. Seal with a clear lacquer sealer. Prime with enamel undercoat. Final-finish with two or three coats of enamel (high or low gloss, as you prefer), sanding well between each coat. For natural finish, use several coats of polyurethane.

HAIR-GROOMING CENTER. Fasten this wall-hung cabinet over a wall outlet, if there is one at a proper height. Otherwise, run heavy-duty extension cord into it from the nearest outlet. Take care to secure the cord to the wall with insulated staples or protec-

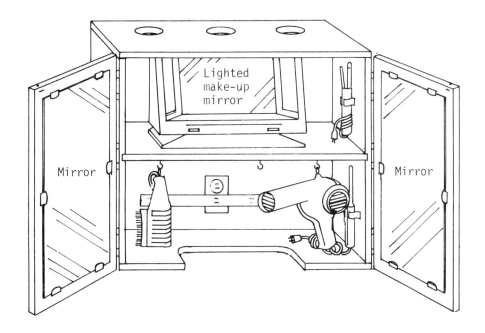

13-2. Hair-grooming center is 32 inches high, 36 inches wide, and 9¹/₄ inches deep, but you can adjust dimensions as you wish.

tive tape. The grooming center is designed to incorporate a strip plug so that the tangle and drag of appliance cords can be kept in some kind of order.

A lighted makeup mirror occupies the top shelf, and the cabinet doors are lined inside with mirrors to provide the convenience of three-way viewing.

The bottom shelf has a shallow cutout to permit close approach. It also aids ventilation, since many appliances are quite warm when put away. Ventilation holes in the top of the cabinet will drain heat given off by the mirror lights.

The interior can be outfitted with hooks and metal clips for holding hair dryers, curling irons, styling sticks, and the like. Overlap doors are butt-hinged to the cabinet.

Material. This cabinet can be made of 1x10 stock or $1/2$-inch plywood. Backing should be of $1/2$ inch plywood since the cabinet will be fastened to the wall by bolts driven from inside it. Or, the back can be attached to wall cleats.

Procedure. Cut dado in verticals for center shelf support. In back edge of center shelf, cut a notch for mirror cord. Make a cut-out in the front edge of the bottom shelf.

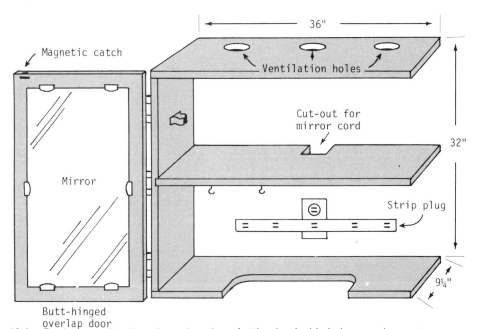

16-3. Partial-assembly view shows location of strip plug inside hair-grooming center.

Butt-join verticals between the top and bottom pieces, glue-nailing into place. Slide the shelf into the dado, securing it with glue and brads driven from the outside.

Fasten the backing into place on the frame and, with a saber or keyhole saw, make a cutout for the wall outlet or extension cord.

Cut and fit doors, attaching them to the cabinet with butt hinges. Install magnetic catch and latches. After final-finishing the cabinet, fasten in door mirrors with surface-mounted clips.

Drill holes in backing through which bolts can be fitted to the wall.

Finish. Sand and seal, then paint or give a natural finish.

14 | Three-in-One Room Divider

A CLOSET, CABINETS, and shelves combine to create this two-section multipurpose storage unit. While designed to be partially accessible from both sides—in its guise as a room divider—the three-in-one can also be placed against the wall if the size of a room or its traffic pattern require it. Moreover, the closet can be outfitted to hold things other than clothing: stereo equipment or china and glassware.

The divider is 24 inches deep (front to back) and 86 inches high overall. (Without the soffit and top horizontal slab, or roof, the case section and closet are $82^1/_2$ inches high.) The case section is 60 inches long and is joined to a small closet made of 2x3s fitted with 30-inch bi-fold doors. The doors require a finished opening $30^1/_2$ inches wide and $80^3/_4$ inches high, making the overall exterior length of the total unit about $93^1/_2$ inches long.

The case section, of plywood slabs, contains shelves, glide-out drawers, and a cabinet with doors. The shelves, of tempered glass, are lit from above by fixtures recessed in the top and concealed by a wrap-around soffit. The room divider can be painted or given a natural finish.

Because of its size, plan to assemble the two-section unit on-site once you've cut and prepared the component parts in your workshop.

Material. Use 4x8x$^3/_4$ birch-faced plywood panels for the $23^1/_4$-inch-wide uprights and horizontals. Doors and drawer fronts should also be of matching birch-faced plywood, although you can use $^1/_2$-inch plywood if you'd rather.

Use stock 2x3s for the closet framework. Soffit strips are of clear, well-seasoned 1x10 lumber. Tops for the case section and the closet, which will have cutouts for downlight fixtures, can be made from a half sheet of the birch-faced plywood but you can, of course, use lesser grade material, even scrap, since it will not be seen when surrounded by the soffit.

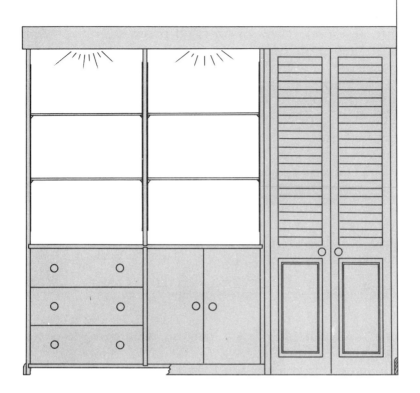

14-1. Three-In-One Room Divider has a closet with bi-fold doors, a cabinet with doors, drawers, and glass shelves. Light filters down from fixtures recessed in the top which is surrounded by a deep soffit strip. Drawer section and closet have solid backings, but door section is designed to be accessible from both sides.

Backings for the closet and case sections can be $1/4$-inch plywood, hardboard, particleboard, or MCP material.

You will need clips and slotted metal pilasters for adjustable shelf supports, tempered $1/4$-inch glass for shelves, drawer extension glides, and downlight fixtures. Plan to have the fixtures wired to two separate control switches, one for the closet, and one on a dimmer for the case section so that light levels here can be adjusted. A steady bright glare shining through the glass can become annoying after awhile.

Procedure. Cut out all case section verticals and horizontals. Cut dadoes so that case members can be fitted together, then dry-assemble the unit so you can check for level and proper fit of dado joints.

Measure and mark locations for shelf pilasters, drawer glides, and door hinges on the partially assembled case section.

Next, measure and cut doors, and check for fit within the case opening. Mark hinge locations on doors, also. Doors can be inset flush within the cabinet opening and hung on pivot hinges (see Chapter 6). Make four doors if you want to make the cabinet accessible from both sides.

Measure, cut, and glue-nail drawers; clamp each one and set aside to dry. Drawers can have false fronts that fit flush within the cabinet opening. Allow for space needed by glides between the drawer sides and the cabinet sides. Install the drawer glides to drawers and cabinet and test the drawers for fit and smooth operation. When the drawers are working properly, disassemble the case section and install shelf pilasters. You may want them in the cabinet section, too, if you want to have adjustable shelving there as well. Set aside case section parts and proceed to the closet framework.

Measure and cut the 2x3s, remembering to allow for a $30^1/_2$x80x$^3/_4$-inch finished opening for the closet doors.

To fashion the closet framework, make two rectangles of 2x3s, one for the top plate, and one for the floor plate. Cut 2x3s for verticals to be nailed between top and bottom rectangles at all four corners when you are ready to assemble the closet framework on-site.

Measure and cut backing material you will use on the closet and case section. Also, measure and cut tops for the closet and case section, making cutouts for lighting fixtures.

Delay cutting the 1x10s for soffit strips until the closet and case section are joined together. There are bound to be small but critical differences in what the dimensions should be and what they actually will be once you've joined the two sections together, out-of-plumb floors and walls being one problem you're most likely to encounter.

Now bundle everything together and move to the site for final assembly.

Assembly. Glue-nail the case section together, including the kick-plate. Clamp or weight and set aside to dry. (*Note:* The existing baseboard will have to be taken into consideration. You can either cut away a portion of it, or cut the closet frame to fit around it.)

Glue-nail all portions of the closet frame together, including cross braces. Since one end of the closet will be against the wall, predetermine the location of an existing wall stud into which you can anchor one of the closet verticals. A 24-inch closet cannot span two studs, so it is well to take advantage of one, at least. Toggle bolts can be used to anchor the other vertical to the existing wall. Countersink these screws and bolts so they cannot interfere with the operation of the door or snag clothing. But do not final-drive these fasteners until the case sections and closet have been

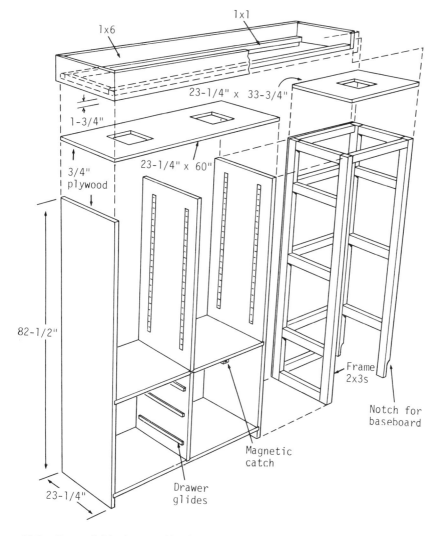

14-2. Room divider is a combination of slab and open-frame constructions and consists of two sections joined together; a closet and case section unified by a wrap-around soffit of 1x10s that slips over the top and hides all joints. The soffit rests on 1x1 cleats attached to its inside surface. The cleat is omitted at the end that butts against the wall, and the 1x6 cut narrower, so the soffit will be flush with the closet.

joined, until shims are in place, and until plumb line and level tell you the full unit is in a square and level position.

Install overhead track for closet doors; also cut away section of the floor plate that is across the door opening. Drill holes in the remaining floor plate and drive and countersink wood screws into the floor.

Shove the completed case section into position against the closet frame and fasten the two sections together with wood screws driven through the end panel into the 2x3s.

Test-hang the closet doors to check for smooth operation, shimming where needed. Plan to final-hang the doors after the wiring

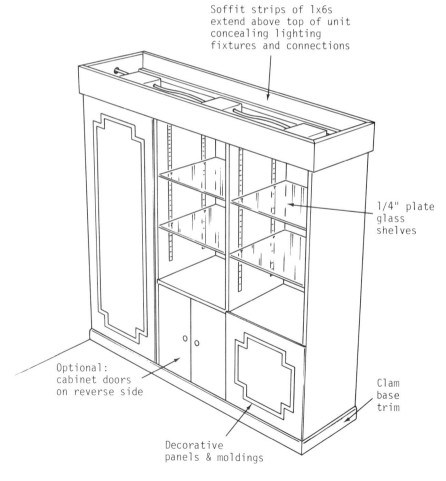

14-3. Reverse side of the room divider shows one way to decorate back of closet and drawer cabinet with shaped panels and molding.

is installed, the closet interior is fitted with shelves, and the divider has been sanded and final-finished.

With nails, fasten cutout tops into position over the case section and closet. Set lighting fixtures in place, and connect wiring to wall switches. Have an electrician do this unless you know exactly what you're doing.

Final-drive all floor and wall anchoring screws and bolts, checking occasionally that the unit remains plumb and square. Next, measure, cut, and miter the ends of the soffit frame that surround the top of the room divider. Glue-nail (or screw) 1x1 cleats to the inside of the soffit frame, $1^3/_4$ inches from the bottom edge (Fig. 14-2, Detail C). Rest the soffit frame members on the cleats and face-nail them to the top of the divider.

Finish. Install clam base trim (or other trim you prefer) around the bottom of the room divider. Sand the case section, drawers, doors, soffit, and exposed closet framework. Fill and cover plywood edges with tape, wood veneer, or spackle, sanding and blending the edges of the edge covering material with the plywood surface veneer. Dust the unit thoroughly with a tack cloth, taking particular care to clean out corners and seams. You can now paint the room divider or give it a natural finish.

In situations where closet and cabinet backings will be visible, you can cover them with paint, fabric, paper, decorative panels and moldings (Fig. 14-3), or give them whatever treatment harmonizes with the color and style of the surroundings.

15 | Storage for a Bed

A CONVENTIONAL BED occupies valuable space that's unused two-thirds of the time. One way to recapture lost floor space is to stand beds upright when they're not needed.

With the remarkable and reliable Murphy Bed spring mechanism that attaches to the floor, you can create a disappearing bed with any size mattress you own. Write Murphy Door Bed Company, 40 East 34th Street, New York, New York 10016 for information and spec sheets. The spring mechanism and support frame can be ordered from the manufacturer and will arrive with all necessary hardware plus assembly and installation instructions.

A fully made-up double bed stands inside this 80x78x22-inch wall system created to look like a single cabinet. Actually, it's a storage shell consisting of two bookcase-like units (9 inches deep) facing inward, and linked by a plywood-slab roof. Its shelves hold everything one needs at bedside. The base of each unit is enclosed and fitted with a hinged top to provide a storage bin for extra bedding.

The shell has no backing. The existing wall serves that purpose and can be left as-is or covered by fabric shirred on rods, quilting stapled to wall, patterned paper—just about anything.

Exterior styling possibilities for the shell's exterior are equally plentiful. Leave it plain and unadorned for a contemporary look. Add moldings and related hardware for an Oriental, French Provincial, Early American or Colonial appearance. Folding doors on shutter hinges are recommended because they stack compactly out of the way when open. Select door style that is compatible with shell exterior.

In selecting a site and cabinetry for concealed beds, keep these dimensions in mind. Stored upright against the wall, a made-up standard-size bed needs a space that's only 19 inches deep. The storage shell here is 22 inches deep simply to permit extra air circulation around mattress and bedding. When a standard 75-inch-long double or single bed is fully extended, the distance from back wall to foot of mattress is 80 inches; 86 inches if the mattress is Queen size.

15-1. Storage shell for Murphy Bed looks like a wall system, but it's actually two bookcase-like units facing inward, linked to a plywood slab roof. Full-size double bed needs an opening 80 inches high and 60 inches wide.

Stored upright, double beds need an opening 80 inches high and 60 inches wide (80x42 inches for single beds; 86x63 inches for Queen size).

Material. Use $^3/_4$-inch birch-faced plywood for the main body of the two vertical units, shelves, and slab roof. Cross braces are of 1x6 stock. Kickplates are of 2x2s so wood screws can be driven through them (and bottom shelf) in order to anchor vertical units to floor.

The bin at the bottom of each unit has an interior frame of $^3/_4$-inch molding strips which will support the hinged top and face panel. The face panel is of $^1/_4$-inch surfaced plywood. (Smoothness is important here so that bedcovers and stored bedding will not snag on bin surfaces.)

Procedure. Cut four end-panel verticals and two back panels. Back panels will fit between end panels. Cut dadoes in the end panels for the fixed top and bottom shelves. Drill peg holes for shelf supports. Cut $^3/_4$-inch molding strips for the bin support frame and nail to verticals. Set nails and fill depressions with wood paste. Sand smooth.

Cut top and bottom shelves, slide into dadoes, and glue-nail in place. With units lying flat, glue-nail backing into place between end panels. Clamp, set aside to dry.

With units upright, install the 2x2 kickplate under the bottom shelf. Drill pilot holes for floor-anchoring screws.

Cut the slab roof, move it and the partially completed shelf units to the site. Here, you can completely assemble and finish the storage shell and install bed mechanism later. (Once you've fastened a simple metal strip to the floor just inside the shell opening, you will final-assemble the bedspring and support system from outside the enclosure.)

Assembly. To avoid having to cope with the existing baseboard, and to assure a snug fit against the wall, cut out a section of the baseboard before you set the storage shell in place. You can reinstall it in the enclosure later, if you want.

Set shelf units in place, 60 inches apart, facing each other. Through predrilled holes in bases of the units, anchor them to the floor with wood screws. If subfloor is masonry, drill holes into it with a masonry drill and insert rawl plugs into each hole; drive screws.

Check with a spirit level as you go along, and shim where necessary to keep shelf units in plumb position.

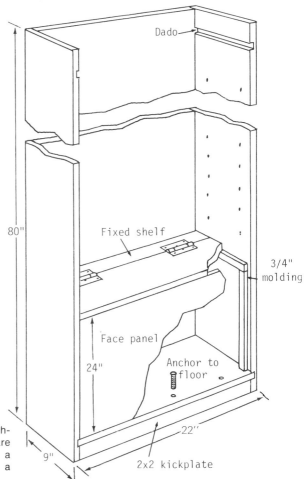

Dado

80"

Fixed shelf

3/4"
molding

Face panel

24"

Anchor to
floor

15-2. End units are built of birch-faced plywood. The uprights are drilled and dadoed for shelves; a hinged shelf midway encloses a storage bin at the bottom.

9"

22"

2x2 kickplate

Glue-nail bin face panel in place. Nail hinged top into place over bin opening.

Fasten top and bottom cross braces to the back edges of the shelf units, using corner iron braces. See detail in Fig. 15-3.

With a helper, set the plywood slab roof into place and nail it to cross brace and top edges of shelf units. Fill seams and gaps with wood paste. Let dry and sand smooth.

If an existing wall outlet is not inside the storage shell, drill a hole or holes in the units for introducing electric cords to power strip plugs for lamps, radio, and other appliances.

Sand, seal, and final-finish interior of the storage shell. Cover and sand exposed plywood edges. Set the shelves on flanged metal peg supports. Cover or decorate the back wall as preferred.

119

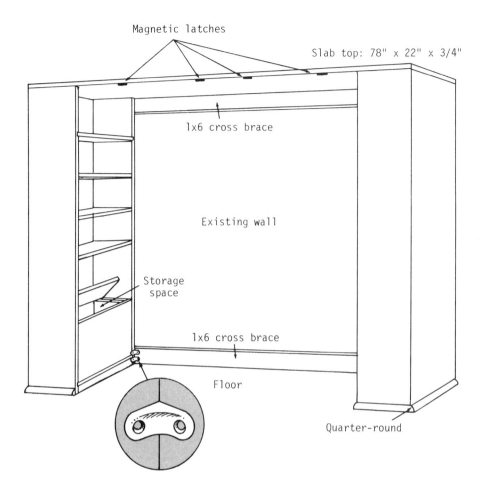

Magnetic latches

Slab top: 78" x 22" x 3/4"

1x6 cross brace

Existing wall

Storage space

1x6 cross brace

Floor

Quarter-round

15-3. End units are joined by a slab top and cross braces. The back is left open. Exterior styling, such as the addition of a crown molding cap, depends on the decor of the room.

Fit and install folding doors, using shutter hinges. Attach magnetic catches to underside of slab roof; attach latches to doors.

Following the manufacturer's instructions, fasten the bed base section to the floor just inside the opening. Attach mattress support and spring mechanism and test for smooth operation. Add your own mattress and store bed in its new storage shell.

Finish. Seal and cover all exposed plywood edges. Sand, seal, and final-finish exterior and all trim. Use paint, stain, or give a natural finish. Add any decorative metal hardware last. For traditional styling, use 6-inch crown molding.

16 | Basement Organizers

ALL THAT SPACE under basement stairs is never wasted. It is filled with stacks of things, all hard to get at. When you want them they're always buried at the back of the heap. Cure the problem with roll-out bins that fit under shelves.

The shelves are enclosed by a basement wall on the far side, and by a curtain-wall of plywood—cut stair-step fashion—on the facing side. Cleats fastened to the existing wall and along the inner edges of the curtain wall support the shelves.

Open stairs without risers should be closed by nailing panels of backing material to the underside of the stringers.

Tall end-wall braces support the highest end of the curtain-wall.

Contents of the tall and middle bins are accessible from an open side, like a drawer set on end. The short bin has an open top.

Material. Bins, shelves, and curtain-wall are of $3/4$-inch plywood. Cleats are of 1x2s. Tall end-wall braces are of 2x4s. Guiderail strips can be of quarter-round wood molding or aluminum angle strips. Use $3/4$-inch molding strips for corner blocks in the small bin, and for shelf supports in taller bins. Under-stair backing for the open stairs can be of $1/4$-inch plywood or particleboard. Use $1/2$-inch plywood backing in the tall and middle bins. Choose non-swivel heavy-duty rubberized casters for the bins.

Procedure. Plan this project to scale on paper first because the angle of the stairs will influence the dimensions of bins, curtain-wall cuts, shelf depth—everything.

First, enclose the underside of the stairway. Then nail the end-wall frame to the floor and stringer.

Cut the curtain-wall by making the stairstep cutouts in panels of plywood. Nail 1x2 shelf-support cleats to the inside of the curtain-wall along its horizontal edges. *Note:* If the curtain-wall has to be pieced in order to form a continuous wall, butt ends of each piece together and join them by a vertical 1x2 strip nailed over the inside seam.

Fasten the curtain-wall to the stringer with nails. Then fasten it to the end-wall brace and to a floor cleat at the base of the stairs.

With spirit level and a length of scrap, determine position of the shelf-support cleats on the existing wall under the stairs. Install cleats with masonry nails or wood screws, depending upon wall material.

Cut the shelves and slide them in place over the cleats.

Make bins to fit under curtain-wall cuts. Allow $1/2$ inch clearance between each bin and the top and sides of the enclosure.

When the casters are installed, set the bins in position under the curtain-wall. Using chalk or tape, determine where on the floor to install the guiderail strips and the stop-strip. Install a stop-strip first. Set it parallel to the wall and a distance out from it. This dis-

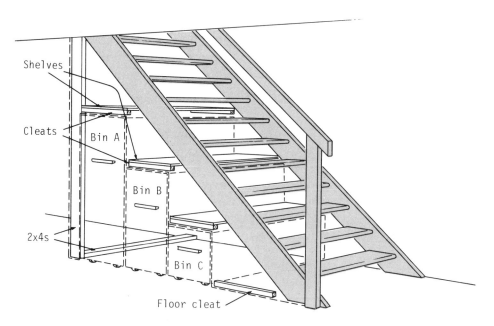

16-1. Roll-out bins fit under a curtain-wall of plywood, cut step-fashion. The space enclosed by the curtain-wall, the stairway, and the existing basement wall is fitted with shelves over each bin. End-wall braces of 2x4s fastened to floor and overhead stringer will support highest end of the the curtain-wall.

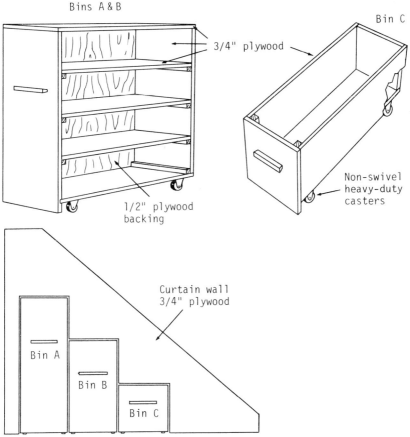

Bins A & B

Bin C

3/4" plywood

1/2" plywood backing

Non-swivel heavy-duty casters

Curtain wall 3/4" plywood

Bin A

Bin B

Bin C

16-2. To prevent sway in taller bins, the backing is $1/2$-inch plywood and the bottom shelf is dadoed to the face panel. The short bin is made entirely of $3/4$-inch plywood, is butt-joined and has corner blocks at the front.

tance is to be 1 inch plus the amount that the bin overhangs its casters at the rear.

Finish. Sand, seal, and paint bins and curtain-wall the same color. Or give all exposed surfaces a natural finish. Install metal pull-bars on facing ends of bins.

17 | One-Wall Garage Organizer

BECAUSE THEY'RE AT ground level and have wide doorways, garages have a wider assortment of things stored in them than basements do. It's not easy hauling spare tires and lawn furniture up and down stairs. More often than not, household accumulations take over and cars stay out in the driveway.

A survey of what people store in their garages and why would occupy a team of psychologists for years. But an informal study suggests there are four categories of things all garages have stored in them: an old but working refrigerator, newspapers and magazines, lawn-care implements, and folding furniture. Of these, newspapers and magazines require more carting around than the others, which are either permanent or seasonal.

When you take into account how much more extra effort is needed to get printed material out of the house than into it, you realize there ought to be a better way. Especially since recycling is a major activity these days, and sanitation departments are demanding that trash be virtually gift-wrapped before they will accept it.

This wall organizer is designed to help bring order and step-saving logic to the routine management of household storage.

Giving the refrigerator position of honor, a system of ladder-like supports and partitions is built around it. Overhead is space for folding furniture and pads. An end section backed with pegboard holds lawn-care tools and related necessities. Shelves hold odds and ends. In the center is a wrapdesk for bundling and tying stacks of paper and cut-down cartons. Under the wrapdesk are plastic cans for sorted glass and metal, ready for recycling pick-up

One end of the wrapdesk extends slightly beyond its partition to overhang a bundle bin parked beside it. Over the desk is pegboard for holding spools of twine, linoleum cutting knife, scissors, tape.

The bundle bin (Fig. 17-3) is designed to be a daily storage container for paper, and the means for transporting it to curbside, all in one. It is a handtruck with sides, and is designed to slope downward when in an at-rest position so the bundles can be easily pushed out.

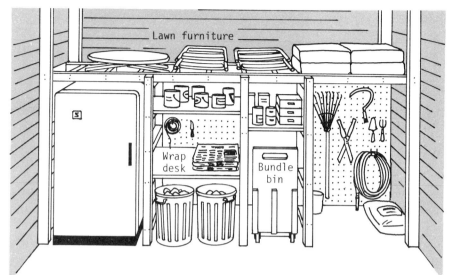

17-1. Garage-wall organizer is for the things almost every garage contains besides a car or two. Wrapdesk next to refrigerator is for tying up bundles of newspapers, magazines, cardboard cartons (cut-down). Wheeled bin next to desk is for storing the bundled paper and for carting it to the curb.

The wall organizer's dimensions have to be determined by the amount of space you have, of course. Except for the refrigerator, all other sections can be as shallow or as wide as you want. The wrapdesk needs to be only big enough to hold a stack of newspapers with a little extra room for handling and tying.

The bundle bin is just slightly larger than a folded newspaper, which measures 16 by 12 inches after it's been handled and refolded. The back, with hand-hold cutout, is 46 inches high but can be more or less depending upon the person who will be pushing the bin forward. A stout metal push-bar can be used instead of the hand-hold.

Material. The system's horizontals and verticals are ladders made of 2x3s. Rib braces for the bundle bin are also of 2x3s. Shelves can be scrap, plywood, or lumber. Shelf supports, and indeed all other supports and anchors, are angle irons, mending plates, L-brackets, and rigid metal L-braces. Wrapdesk top is of $^3/_4$-inch plywood surfaced with a piece of resilient vinyl flooring installed with contact adhesive. The bundle bin is of $^3/_4$-inch plywood, birch-faced both sides (to avoid splinters).

Procedure. Measure and cut 2x3s for ladder sides and cross braces (Fig. 17-2). Make as many ladders as the space will accept and the number of sections your organizer will contain. Ladders

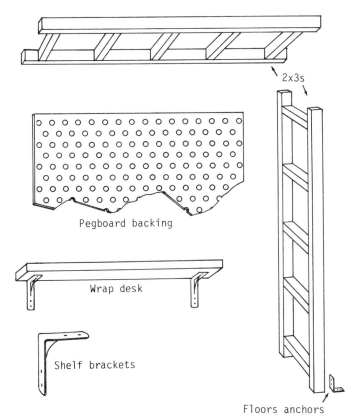

17-2. Basic framework for the garage-wall organizer is composed of a series of ladders, made of 2x3s. Shelves, pegboard, and wrapdesk supply plenty of extra storage and work space. Supports and connectors for the complete unit are ordinary mending plates, L-brackets, rigid metal L-braces.

need not have special joints. Butt-joining cross braces between verticals with nails or wood screws will do.

Place the ladders into position to form a full-wall framework. Anchor the ladders to each other and to the existing wall, floor, overhead garage framework. Use angle irons, mending plates, and fasteners that are suitable for the kind of materials being joined.

Cut the pegboard for the wrapdesk backing and the garden implement sections. Snap spacers to the back of the pegboard and anchor the panels to the garage wall, or the 2x3 verticals.

Cut shelf lengths and anchor between the verticals with L-brackets.

Cut the wrapdesk top, smooth exposed edges. Install rigid metal shelf supports to the verticals in wrapdesk section. Fasten one desktop to supports with screws driven from the underside. Aim for level, firm work surface at a comfortable height. Position the top so there is a slight overhang at the end next to the bundle bin. Cut resilient vinyl floorcovering (sheet or tile) and attach to the top with contact adhesive. Clean excess adhesive off, cover the top with a wide piece of scrap material and add weights to promote a firm bond.

The bundle bin. Cut ³/₄-inch plywood for high-back, bottom, and angled sides (Fig. 17-3). Cut hand-hold in back. Clamp and glue-nail back to bottom. Clamp and glue-nail side panels into place.

Cut rib braces of 2x3s. Nail bottom ribs to underside of bin at its sides and in the middle. Join back ribs to bottom ribs and to unit's back panel. Use glue and screws. Attach 5-inch swivel casters to bottom ribs.

Finish. Since appearance is not a big factor, you can sand and seal the wood and let it go at that. To make the birch-faced plywood bin more wear-resistant, use paint or clear shellac.

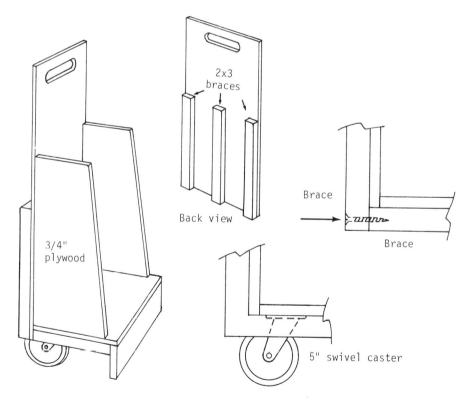

17-3. Bundle bin is 46 inches high, 17¹/₂ inches wide, and 12 inches deep. It holds stack of bundled scrap paper neatly in one place, and is used to move it outside for trash pickup.

18 | Attic Organizers

FINDING WAYS to use attic space to the best advantage is not always easy. What space exists is oddly shaped; few ready-made storage structures ever fit. The two projects here are designed to provide simplified storage places for those awkward shapes one finds under the roof—be it one with a high center peak or one with very low clearance.

HATCHWAY STORAGE SURROUND. Low-clearance attics reached via pull-down ladder present special problems. Only the space within reach around the open hatchway is available for storing things. Objects at the back of the crowd tend to get pushed back under the eaves. To keep your possessions from straying too far away, put them in a series of step-shaped boxes that surround the hatchway opening (Fig. 18-1).

The boxes can have shelves and vertical partitions spaced according to what you plan to store in them. One or more of the boxes can have openings in the backing through which long objects can protrude.

If dust-proofing is a factor, the faces of the boxes can be covered with flaps of clear vinyl held in place with Velcro® tape. See Fig. 18-3.

Material. Use ¹/₂-inch softwood plywood since finish and appearance are not important considerations. Backing and partitions can be ¹/₄-inch material, either plywood or particleboard. Shelves can be ¹/₂-inch plywood. Shelves and partitions are supported by ¹/₂-inch molding strips surface mounted where needed.

Procedure. First, measure and plan in advance to be sure finished boxes will fit through the hatchway opening.

Cut the end panels; make six of these. Cut top #1; make three. Cut top #2; make three. Cut backing #1; make three. Cut backing #2; make three. Cut bottoms; make three. Cut shelves and partitions.

Mark shelf positions on the inside face of the end panels and nail in the shelf support cleats.

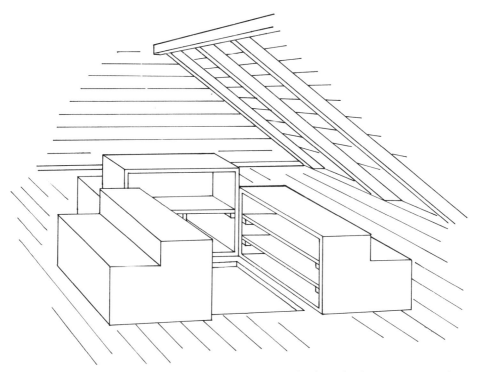

18-1. Hatchway storage surround for low clearance attics is a simple arrangement of three step-shaped boxes designed to keep your possessions within easy reach.

Join the end panels to their tops and backings in this order: Nail backing #1 into place. Then top #1. Nail top #2 into place. Then backing #2. Turn the unit on its side and nail the bottom into place. Fill seams and gaps with wood filler. When dry, sand smooth.

Mark positions for partitions, nail molding strips into place on bottom and onto underside of shelves or top. Slide shelves into

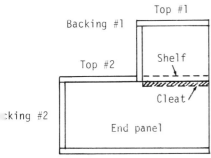

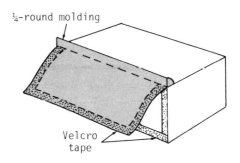

18-2. Step-boxes for hatchway surround are built as shown. Dust-proofing flap of clear vinyl can cover entire opening of a step-box, or just a portion of it.

place and nail to their cleats. Place partitions against their support cleats and nail.

If dustproof clear vinyl flaps are to be used, sand the raw edges of the box opening and seal with several coats of primer. Glue Velcro strips to box edges across the bottom and sides. Cut vinyl flap and glue (or sew) Velcro receiving strip along the sides and bottom. Fasten vinyl flap across the top of the box opening with heavy contact tape or by a strip of molding held in place with brads.

Finish. Sand, seal, and finish either with paint or stain or even decorative paper.

ATTIC DORMITORY TOWER OF CUBES. Under roofs with a high center peak there is enough space for a storage tower of open-face cubes which can act as headboards for two to four 30-inch-wide beds. Here is vertical storage as well as a dormitory for young guests.

The tower is composed of a base of eight 16-inch cubes (four cubes on top of four cubes), and a setback formed by four 12-inch cubes, and a tower-top effect of one see-through 12-inch cube.

The open ends of the cubes can face in any direction. The closed sides can be painted different colors.

Overall dimensions of the assembled tower will be 56x32x32 inches.

Material. Use $^3/_4$-inch plywood, softwood or hardwood, depending on how rustic or sleek you want the tower to look.

Procedure. Taking into account the $^3/_4$-inch thickness of the material that all parts of the cube will have, cut sides and bottom in dimensions that will produce an equal-sided structure when all the parts are assembled. The method of building a cube is explained in Chapter 5. For easy reference, the drawing in that chapter is repeated here, along with dimensions for building cubes of different sizes.

Cube assembly. Apply glue to edges of the Sides that will butt against the Back. Set the Back and two Side pieces into position on the Bottom piece and shove the whole thing against a wall or other firm vertical surface to steady your work. Fasten the Side pieces to the Back by nailing through the Back.

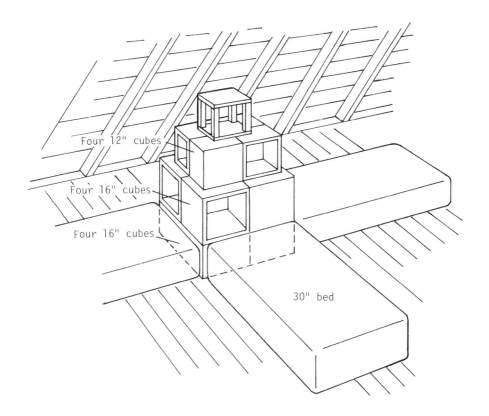

18-4. Attic dormitory tower of cubes serve as headboards for 30-inch beds and as compartmented vertical storage that is accessible from different directions and levels. Open cube tower-top is optional.

For 16-inch cube
Cut 2 for Top and Bottom 16″ x 16″ x ³/₄″
Cut 1 for Back 14¹/₂″ x 16″ x ³/₄″
Cut 2 for Sides 14¹/₂″ x 15¹/₄″ x ³/₄″
For 12-inch cube
Cut 2 for Top and Bottom 12″ x 12″ x ³/₄″
Cut 1 for Back 10¹/₂″ x 12″ x ³/₄″
Cut 2 for Sides 10¹/₂″ x 11¹/₄″ x ³/₄″
For open 12-inch cube
Cut 2 for Top and Bottom 12″ x 12″ x ³/₄″
Cut 4 for posts 10¹/₂″ high from 2x2 stock

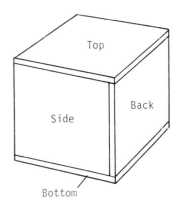

18-5. How basic cube is built.

Apply glue to the top edges of Sides and Back and set the Top in place across them. Tapping where needed to keep the corners square, nail through the Top into the edges of the Sides and Back. Turn the unit upside down and apply glue to all exposed edges. Fit the Bottom into place and nail. Set aside to dry and weight the unit with books or other heavy objects.

Fill gaps and seams with wood filler. Let dry and sand smooth. Give the cubes a final finish and carry them to attic. Arrange them to form a tower, having open ends of cubes placed as needed for access from various directions.

The open cube is simply for effect, therefore is optional.

Finish. Sand, seal, and finish either with paint or stain or even decorative paper.

Index